TM

HONORABLE
EMPLOYEE
HANDBOOK

CITADEL PRESS
Kensington Publishing Corp.
www.kensingtonbooks.com

CITADEL PRESS BOOKS are published by

Kensington Publishing Corp.
850 Third Avenue
New York, NY 10022

All Kensington titles, imprints, and distributed lines are available at special quantity discounts for bulk purchases for sales promotions, premiums, fund-raising, educational, or institutional use. Special book excerpts or customized printings can also be created to fit specific needs. For details, write or phone the office of the Kensington special sales manager: Kensington Publishing Corp., 850 Third Avenue, New York, NY 10022, attn: Special Sales Department; phone 1-800-221-2647.

CREDITS

Design & Layout: Michael "Aeon" Fiegel

Writing: Michael Fiegel, Ken Lustig, Corey Mosher, except for pp. 44–45, Lee Garvin

Editing: Alex Conde, Christa Perez, Jen Schoonover

Translations: Fuyugare no Keshiki, Pedro Mele

Illustrations: D.J. Coffman, Rocco Commisso, Fil Kearney, Abby Perry, Colin Throm

Ninja Burger Logo: Ken Lustig

Thanks to: BizFu, Steve Jackson Games, Fark, 9th Level Games, and all of our many fans.

First printing: June 2006

10 9 8 7 6 5 4 3 2 1

Printed in the United States of America

Library of Congress Control Number: 2005938603

ISBN 0-8065-2796-X

CONTENTS

Greetings, prospective new Ninja Burger employee:

You are about to embark on the job of a lifetime. Never again will you work in a more thrilling, exciting, fast-paced, challenging career field. Never again. Because if you even TRY to work somewhere else after this, you will be hunted down and killed.

Please take a moment to to fill out the New Employee Information Card below, and submit a photocopy to the Ninja Archive Division as soon as possible. The information you provide on this card will assist us in notifying your next of kin and/or identifying your body, should it become necessary.

Odds are, it will.

We hope you enjoy working for Ninja Burger, however brief your stay. Keep this *Honorable Employee Handbook* with you at all times – the information within its pages may just save your life some day. Also, it makes a handy coaster.

Domo Arigato,

MIchael "aeon" Fiegel,
Ninja Burger Employee Resources
Ninja Archive Division (N.A.D.)
aeon@ninjaburger.com

NEW EMPLOYEE INFORMATION CARD

Name: _____
Address: _____
City: _____ State: _____
Postal Code: _____ Country: _____
Gender: _____ Date of Birth: _____
Hair Color: _____ Eye Color: _____
Height: _____ Weight: _____

Next of Kin: _____
Address: _____
City: _____ State: _____
Postal Code: _____ Country: _____

Official Use Only
EID:
SSN:
PDQ:
TMI:
TTFN:

仲間に加わりたいという人がいたら、たとい信仰の弱い人であっても、あたたかく迎え入れなさい。 事の良し悪しについて考えが違うからといって、批判してはいけません。 たとえば、偶像に供えられた肉を食べてもよいかどうかなどと、議論してはいけません。あなたがたは、偶像に供えられた肉を食べても別に悪くはない、と信じているかもしれません。 しかし、ほかの人たちの信仰は、もっと弱いのです。 彼らは、偶像に供えられた肉を食べるのは悪いとして、全く肉なしですませ、肉類よりむしろ野菜を食べるほうがよいと思っています。 肉を食べてもよいと思っている人は、食べようとしない人を見下してはいけません。 また、食べようとしない人は、食べる人を非難してはいけません。神様はそのどちらをも受け入れて、自分の子供としてくださったからです。 4どちらも神様に仕えているのであって、あなたに仕えているわけではありません。 神様に対して責任を負うのであって、あなたに責任を負うのではありません。 正しいか、まちがっているかは、神様がその人に教えてくださるはずです。 しかも神様は、その人が正しく行動できるように助けることがおできになります。

Kensori Mishko
Ninja Burger cofounder

*A*ssuming you survive basic training, I'd like to welcome you to the Ninja Burger team. Remember, there is no "I" in TEAM but there is an "i" in ninja—as well as a "j," which is sort of like an "i", but with a curvy bottom.

However, there are definitely no "i's" in burger, which is how we like to keep it, especially since the problem we had that one time with the health inspector.

Kenshiro Aette
Ninja Burger cofounder

P.S. Go ahead and use one of those handwriting fonts when you paste this into the Handbook so it looks like we actually wrote it. And be sure to remove this note before you go to press.

1: ANYONE, ANYTIME, ANYWHERE

Ninja Burger™ is 100 percent devoted to delivering "Triple A" service to our customers. We will deliver to <u>anyone</u> in the world, <u>anytime</u> and <u>anywhere</u>.

ANYONE: Ninja Burger has no political/religious affiliations or allegiances. We will deliver to anyone who requests our service (if they have good credit). We also will not share our customer list or customer information with anyone else, for any reason. You stick to politics—we'll stick to delivering food.

ANYTIME: Ninja Burger is open 24 hours a day, 7 days a week, 365 days a year (366 during leap years). We have facilities in all time zones and hemispheres and are capable of providing 30-minute-or-less service to anywhere on the surface of the earth.[1] Delivery times to locations in geosynchronous orbit will be based on GMT.

ANYWHERE: Ninja Burger has approximately 10,000 locations in most major cities in all 50 United States (including Alaska and Hawaii, but excepting Detroit)[2], and most of Mexico and Canada, as well as parts of Europe and Japan. There's also that one store in Antarctica that we can't talk about.

As part of an aggressive campaign to achieve total world domination[3], Ninja Burger has plans to open more franchises across Eastern Europe, South and Central Asia, Africa, and South America within the next few years.

Please consult the following map; dark areas indicate local coverage.

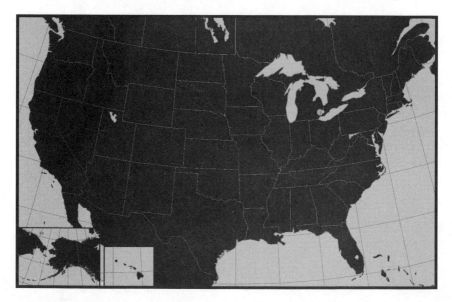

1 Additional delivery charges may apply in some areas, not to exceed $10,000 in most cases.
2 No, not Detroit. Anything but Detroit.   3 Well, at least we're honest about it.

MISSION STATEMENT
Guaranteed delivery in 30 minutes or less or we commit seppuku.

WHAT THAT MEANS TO CUSTOMERS: Hot, fast, and fresh food, flame broiled in the traditions of our honored ancestors—delivered _on_ time, _all_ the time, without fail.

WHAT THAT MEANS TO ENEMIES: Certain destruction if they do not surrender. When we say burger wars, we mean burger wars. No other fast-food chain has Dim-Mak death touch, and we are not afraid to use it.

WHAT THAT MEANS TO EMPLOYEES: Honor, prestige, promotions, and plenty of good benefits.[4]

ARE YOU RIGHT FOR NINJA BURGER?
We are always looking for qualified candidates to join our team, but we won't take just anyone. How do you know if you're the right sort of person for this job? Here are a few qualifications we look for:

- Positive attitude
- Team player
- Like challenge
- Kill with single touch
- Criminal record not a problem

There's a reason we're the number one clandestine fast-food delivery service: We eliminate all who oppose our clan, as well as all undesirable candidates! We guarantee that if we won't take you, no one else will. Ever.

4 In the event of failure to adhere to the Ninja Burger mission statement, a check in an amount equal to the employee's base pay rate times 31 minutes will be delivered to their next of kin.

NINJA BURGER

HISTORY 101

How exactly did a company like Ninja Burger come into existence? Let's take a fun little look through history. Please note that you will be expected to know all this for your final exam—no skipping ahead!

HISTORY OF THE NINJA

The earliest written reference to ninja places them in action as early as 1338, but it was not until the sixteenth century that ninja truly came into their own, during Japan's war-torn Sengoku era. These ninja were tricksters and spies, assassins and bodyguards, who worked tirelessly for the era's most powerful generals (not counting naps).

The best known ninja, Hattori "Devil" Hanzo, was born in 1541 and by the age of sixteen had distinguished himself in battle. He went on to serve several masters, ultimately saving the life of Shogun Tokugawa Ieyasu—founder of the Tokugawa dynasty and arguably the most powerful man in Japan.

Hanzo would serve as a bodyguard for the shogun until his death on December 4, 1596, but his legacy would not die with him. Hanzo was succeeded by his son, Masanari, whose own son succeeded him, and so on through the ages. Their offspring served in battle until the early Edo period (1603–1867), when peace settled and ninja lost focus. In other words, they got bored.

In 1853, the American Commodore Perry established limited trade routes with Japan, which opened fully in 1868 with the restoration of Emperor Meiji to power. It was at this time that ninja, who had dwelled in secret for hundreds of years, rediscovered their focus. Contrary to popular belief, it had nothing to do with waling on guitars.

HISTORY OF FAST FOOD

Thomas Jefferson introduced the U.S. to its first "fast-food" staple in the late 1700s—Belgian-made "potatoes, fried in the French manner" (in other words, "frenched" or "french fries"). Soda pop appeared in 1835 with America's first bottled soda water; the first cola was introduced in 1881, complete with cocaine. It's true.

By the early 1800s, the hamburger was prepared in a variety of styles. A menu from 1836 described a "hamburger steak"—one of the most expensive items on the menu, at 10¢ each. It was not until 1891 that Oscar Weber Bilby of Tulsa, Oklahoma, first thought to put a ground beef patty between two buns, thereby creating the hamburger sandwich. Heinz® ketchup (1876) and French's® mustard (1904) also appeared on the scene, meaning that all the fixings for the staple fast-food meal were in place (except for the Styrofoam).

In 1921, White Castle® appeared in Wichita, Kansas, followed by Big Boy® (1938). However, it was not until the late 1940s when the fast-food concept really hit, with McDonald's® appearing in 1948, followed by Jack in the Box® (1951), Burger King® (1954), Carl's Jr.® (1956), and Wendy's® (1969). The ground was set for Ninja Burger's arrival.

4

HISTORY OF NINJA BURGER

In the midst of all this clamor, Ninja Burger was founded very quietly in 1954. This was almost the company's downfall. Whereas other fast-food restaurants were quite happy to advertise themselves publicly, Ninja Burger required stealth and discretion. The problem was obvious: No one knew Ninja Burger existed. Hence, no customers.

However, Hattori Hanzo's descendants would not give up so easily.

Ninja Burger's big break came in 1962, with John Kennedy and Nikita Khrushchev facing off over the Cuban missile crisis. Neither man had eaten for days. The world stood on the brink of total annihilation, with two powerful, hungry men locked within highly secured vaults. No one in, no one out.

Well, almost no one.

Though the receipts from that first high-profile Ninja Burger delivery are lost, legend holds that Khrushchev ordered his with extra pickle, no onions, and Kennedy got a Combo meal (and a tall leggy blonde).

Ninja Burger's management realized that during this cold war era, they could defeat the other fast-food empires by focusing on the elite—those who truly desired the quick service of a fast-food meal, but were in situations that made it impossible to get what they wanted.

Throughout the '50s, '60s, and '70s, they focused on serving the needs of presidents, executives, kings, The King, Hollywood stars, and astronauts headed for the stars; all those who wanted nothing more than quick service, great food, and ultimate discretion.

NINJA BURGER TODAY

In the late 1970s, Ninja Burger's technicians (along with Al Gore) helped to develop what would become known as the Internet, seeing the new networking tool as a quick, efficient means to coordinate activity around the world. Orders came blazing fast.

And as the Internet grew, so did the potential for expanding Ninja Burger's customer base. Ninja Burger was able to extend their reach to more countries.

The biggest change came in 1999 on the dawn of the new millennium, when Ninja Burger's management decided to once again alter their focus. Building an ultra-secure Web site, they maintained the ninja's stealth and anonymity online while still providing hot, fast, and fresh service to their customers.

Now it is not just the elite that can enjoy a hot and tasty Ninja Burger; it's everyone in the world.[5]

---

5 Except Detroit. Anything but Detroit.[6]
6 If you still don't get this, go rent *Kentucky Fried Movie*.

PUBLIC PERCEPTION OF THE NINJA

As far as the public is concerned, a ninja is a mythical assassin who can skip through the treetops, walk on water, pass through walls, fly into the clouds, and kill his enemies with a single touch by stopping their hearts.

We could point out that ninja didn't wear black, many ninja were samurai (complete with daisho), most ninja didn't use nunchaku, but some did use guns, etc. But there's always someone out there who claims to know better. So rather than fight stereotypes, we prefer to use them to our advantage—they put enemies at a disadvantage and keep our customers interested.

And for those who still think that ninja don't exist, well . . . officially we don't. So no problem.

NINJA MOVIES

The modern public's idea of what a ninja is comes mostly from ninja movies. Most of these ninja films fall into one of two categories:

1. Early ninja films (from the '60s through the mid '80s) made the ninja out to be a warrior with mystical powers. Movies of this era can be identified by words like "American," "Ninja," "Death," and "Master."[7]
2. Later ninja films (from the mid '80s onward) poke fun at the ninja, making him out to be a cartoon or a buffoon. Look for words like "Teenage," "Rangers," "Beverly Hills," "Power," and "Tortoises."

[7] The best of which is the little-known *American Ninja Death Master of Ninja Death*, which went straight to DVD. Unfortunately for this lost classic, this was before the invention of DVDs.

The Public Eye

While it serves our purposes to keep the myths of the ninja alive, it's also important to let our customers know that we exist. If we're too stealthy and secretive, then they won't be able to find us at all, and then we'd be out of business.

And from there, it's pretty much all downhill, really.

You WILL experience the Ninja Burger difference!

About | Food | Jobs | Fun | Locations | Gear

Guaranteed delivery in 30 minutes or less, or we commit Seppuku!

Be sure to read the NB Crew, updated (mostly) weekly!

忍者バーガー

Ninja Burger, anthrenot FORGE and their logos are © and ™ 1999-2005 anthrenot FORGE.

The Web Site

As mentioned earlier, the Ninja Burger Web site was created as a portal to help customers locate our services more easily. Aside from giving people a way to order food, the Web site also allows people to apply for a job, purchase Ninja Burger gear and equipment from our store, and learn about the history of our company—or at least as much as we want to share.

The Web site also features a number of games, puzzles, several weekly comic strips, and other fun diversions for kids, as a way of getting our future customers hooked early.[8] You're never too young to enjoy Ninja Burger![9]

The one thing our Web site does not feature is paid advertisements. Ninja Burger will always remain paid banner and pop-up free. We occasionally feature banners from our friends and partners but ad space is not for sale!

Commercials

Ninja Burger operated for many years before we finally agreed that hiring some marketing specialists was a necessary evil. And one of the first things they told us to do was to purchase advertising space. What a concept!

Obviously one of the major hurdles we needed to overcome was the fact that ninja require absolute secrecy to protect their identities. Thus far, we've managed to maintain their privacy by hiring actors to play all the ninja in our ads—and then killing them, of course. You can never be too sure.

Like every fast-food chain, Ninja Burger has found it helpful to advertise on television and radio.[10] In all these areas we've found it extremely helpful to purchase lower-cost, off-peak advertising, generally between the hours of midnight and six A.M. Research has found that it's during this time that most of our potential customers are either working the late shift, tooling around on the Internet, or lying awake and wondering whether or not the pot roast in the fridge is still good to eat.

For a sample of one of our commercials, please see the next page.

8 One of the few things we'll give other industries credit for coming up with.
9 Consult with your pediatrician before feeding Ninja Burger to children under the age of three.
10 But never in movie theaters. Seriously, who came up with that idea? We hate that.

NINJA BURGER

NINJA BURGER :30 COMMERCIAL

INT. NINJA BURGER LOBBY AREA—DAY
A customer walks into the empty lobby and steps up to the counter.

                  ANNOUNCER
      At Ninja Burger, we believe in the qualities of
      good customer service, a friendly attitude . . .

The customer looks confused, and turns to look over his shoulder.
When he looks back, there is a cashier standing there. The cashier
is dressed head to toe in black ninja garb, including mask. His
name tag reads "Hi, my name is Toshiro."

                  ANNOUNCER
      . . . And total secrecy and stealth at all times.

INT. NINJA BURGER GRILL AREA—DAY
The grill area is empty. Some burgers sizzle on the grill. From
the top of the frame a ninja reaches down and flips the burgers.

                  ANNOUNCER
      Each and every Ninja Burger is flame broiled in
      the traditions of our ancestors, which means
      that every burger we serve is hot and tasty.

INT. NINJA BURGER FRENCH FRY AREA—DAY
The fry area is just a few vats of bubbling grease off to one side
of the grill area. Flames leap up in the background.

                  ANNOUNCER
      And who could forget our world famous French
      Fries of Our Ancestors, cooked hot and tasty
      in the rendered fat of our slain enemies.

A ninja shoves a dismembered arm into a vat of hot french fries.

INT. NINJA BURGER LOBBY AREA—DAY
Customers mill about, carrying bags towards the door.

                  ANNOUNCER
      So come to Ninja Burger today, and see why
      millions of people every day eat the Ninja way.

                BLACK LOGO FRAME
Ninja Burger logo on black background, with "You WILL Discover the
Ninja Burger Difference, or you will DIE," written beneath.

                  ANNOUNCER
      Ninja Burger. No other fast-food
      chain has Dim-Mak death touch.

Stamp "Guaranteed" on logo frame.

FADE TO BLACK

FUN AND GAMES

Since quite a significant number of our potential customers are fond of playing games, one of the most successful avenues for Ninja Burger has been our pursuit of nontraditional advertising vehicles, such as the role-playing game and card game markets.

Not only are our partnerships with game companies such as 9th Level Games and Steve Jackson Games beneficial in building customer lists, but it's a good way to screen those customers; if they can afford $10 or $20 for a game then they can afford to order a burger from us.

PRINT ADVERTISEMENTS

No ad campaign would be complete without some glossy full-page print ads in popular magazines and newspapers—which is why our advertising campaign is not complete.[11] For some reason print doesn't work well for us.

This ad is an example of one of our trial efforts. Shortly after it ran, our marketing department decided to reword our mission statement to use the word "seppuku," as audiences seemed to react better to food imagery when the word "entrails" did not accompany it.

Guaranteed Delivery in 30 Minutes or Less, or We Ritually Disembowel Ourselves and Spill Our Bloody Entrails to Regain Honor.

Order online at http://www.NinjaBurger.com

---

[11] It's also why our marketing department has such a high turnover rate.

NINJA BURGER

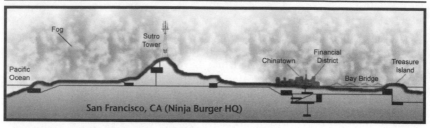

San Francisco, CA (Ninja Burger HQ)

NINJA BURGER HEADQUARTERS

Ninja Burger Headquarters is located below the site of the first Ninja Burger franchise at ▮▮▮▮▮▮▮▮▮▮▮▮▮▮▮▮ San Francisco, California.

The original facility is small, consisting of a 20-seat dining room, a tiny kitchen, a unisex bathroom, and an employee break room. The subterranean facilities are more extensive and include: a kitchen capable of staffing over 100 ninja; an employee gymnasium; training rooms, locker rooms and showers; a 100-bed infirmary; twin helipads; weapons development facilities; a 50-vehicle garage; and a cutting-edge, central dispatch center that coordinates Ninja Burger activities around the world.

In addition to 1,700 cooks, mechanics, drivers, and deliverators, the facility employs 1,000 support personnel, including physicians, trainers, babysitters, massage therapists, animal handlers, janitorial staff, beauticians, and other miscellaneous administrators and managers.

At any given time, some 600 new ninja students are training at the facility, approximately 5 percent of whom will go on to become full-fledged Ninja Burger employees. The other 95 percent will simply go "missing."[12]

NONDISCLOSURE AGREEMENT

As a Ninja Burger employee, you are to keep confidential all information related to the operation of Ninja Burger. This includes but is not limited to: Ninja Burger recipes, delivery routes, customer lists, operational procedures, sales figures, secret handshakes, and other technological and trade secrets. You are also required at all times to keep your involvement as a Ninja Burger employee confidential.

Should you reveal any information about Ninja Burger (including your true identity) to any non-Ninja Burger employee, you will be immediately terminated. And we don't mean fired. While some companies require you to sign a form stating you will not betray them, Ninja Burger employs a much simpler system: If you betray us, we will hunt you down.

Reading any part of this employee guide indicates your acceptance of this nondisclosure agreement, and acknowledgment of the penalties for failure to adhere to it. Not that there's much you can do about it now, since this nondisclosure agreement is on page ten.

---

12 Anyone curious about where these individuals have gone "missing" will be invited to join them immediately. Please be sure to fill out the "next-of-kin" information in your employee packet before asking, however.

HONORABLE EMPLOYEE HANDBOOK

RECRUITMENT AND HIRING POLICIES

EQUAL OPPORTUNITY EMPLOYER

Ninja Burger is an equal opportunity employer. All company policies will be implemented without regard to age, height, weight, race, creed, color, national origin, religion, gender, sexual preference, marital status, ancestry, gender identity, pregnancy, physical or mental disability, medical condition, citizenship, status as a veteran, or political affiliation, with the following exceptions:

- Samurai (dishonorable dogs)
- Pirates (obvious)
- Terrorists (they lack honor!)
- People who own *Gymkata* on VHS (sad, really)
- T. Burke of Tampa, FL (he owes us money)

SELECTION CRITERIA FOR RECRUITMENT

While Ninja Burger will take just about anyone (we have high turnover), we prefer to hire relatives (especially descendants of our founders) as they need less training and are less likely to ~~be killed during~~ fail out of basic training.

Such preferred employees should (in descending order of preference):

1. Be a ninja
2. Be related to a ninja
3. Desire to be a ninja one day
4. Sort of look like a ninja
5. Be able to pronounce "ninja"
6. Be named Tetsuo or something

Ninja recruitment managers should be aware that not everyone who claims to be ninja really is ninja. Be on the lookout for ninja imposters. Can you tell which of the following individuals is really ninja?

The correct answer, of course, is none of them. The real ninja is invisible.

Ninja Burger

Hiring Constraints

Ninja Burger would technically like to hire everyone, but unfortunately there are some "laws" and "regulations" we have to follow in order to keep our license, blah, blah, blah, blah . . .

Accommodation for Disabilities

There's no such thing as disabled at Ninja Burger. There's only ninja-abled. Ninja Burger does not hold disability to be a factor in any company decision, so employees are expected to not hold their own disabilities as a factor.

All ninja, being ninja, are expected to perform tasks with ninja precision and skill, no matter what, including the loss of fingers, limbs, nonvital organs, eyesight, hearing, sanity, significant amounts of blood, etc.[13] Since ninja employees are expected to perform their tasks equally well if they suffer such ailments during the course of employment, they are likewise expected to perform up to par if they are hired in the same condition. Ninja are ninja.

For those who require them, accommodations are available at all franchises and, upon request, will be provided (e.g., wheelchair-accessible vehicles, braille menus, etc.). But real ninja do not need assistance.[14]

Foreign Nationals

Employment of foreign nationals (J-1, H-1, F-1, or permanent resident status) within the United States will be in accordance with federal law and INS regulations. There will be absolutely no exceptions. Wink, wink.

Age Constraints

In accordance with the most stringent state laws, Ninja Burger requires work permits for all persons under the age of eighteen. Furthermore, those individuals who are under the age of sixteen will not be permitted to work in the kitchen or go on deliveries, and will instead be given more age-appropriate tasks.

Yes, this means cleaning the bathrooms. But never fear for your honor, young ninja! Serving Ninja Burger customers is always honorable, even if it is stinky.

---

13 Please note that in the event of loss of one's head (literally, not figuratively) or other vital life-sustaining organs, one will not be expected nor required to continue to perform Ninja Burger duties.
14 Consider blind master swordsman Zatiachi, who delivered a burger and fries through 200 enemy samurai in under thirty minutes and returned with the head of their leader. Or Sensei Tsing, born without limbs, who developed the Flopping Tortoise ninja-fighting style at the age of nineteen, and went on to become one of our best deliverators.

HIRING PROCESS

1. Prospect fills out an application form.
2. Prospect interviewed by personnel ninja.
3. Ninja Resources checks background, etc.
4. Prospect offered a job.
5. Prospect enters into Ninja training.
6. Survivors are Ninja Burger employees.

1. APPLICATION FORM

Applications (see Appendix) must be filled out completely[15] as a sign of commitment to work for Ninja Burger. You may not back out once you sign. Ninja Burger may choose to terminate you at any time. Before you are hired, for example.

2. INTERVIEW

One of our ninja managers will interview the candidate and review his or her application and résumé, asking questions such as:

- What makes you think you're cut out to be a ninja?
- Do you think if you were a real ninja you could catch a throwing star?
- Didn't think I'd really throw it, did you?
- I bet that hurts, doesn't it?
- OK, let's continue. See this katana? Do you think a real ninja could . . .

3. REFERENCES AND BACKGROUND CHECKS

We don't require proof of identity (we know who you are) but sometimes we will call your references to tell them you have recently died and see if they liked you or not. People are a lot more open when they think you're dead. And if we turn you down, well, we've already taken care of business for you.

4. JOB OFFER

Chosen candidates are offered a job with Ninja Burger. Specifics such as exempt/nonexempt status, working hours, pay, and benefits are dealt with later in this handbook. Candidates who refuse a job after being offered one, are—well, let's just say accepting the offer is a healthier proposition.

5. NINJA TRAINING (See page 15)

6. SURVIVORS ARE NINJA BURGER EMPLOYEES

(See page 53)

---

[15] When listing assassinations, claiming JFK or Hoffa—while funny—will result in immediate rejection: We know who did the former, and the latter is still a valued customer.

"TRAIN WELL, MY YOUNG NINJA. FOR IN THE END, THERE CAN BE ONLY ONE.

OR POSSIBLY TWO. THAT'S HAPPENED AT LEAST A FEW TIMES AS I RECALL.

AND I GUESS THREE ISN'T OUT OF THE QUESTION, COME TO THINK OF IT.

FOUR, TOPS."

—SENSEI HAI-LIN DAR

2: BASIC TRAINING

You've survived the hiring process and made it to Ninja basic training. For the next two to six weeks, you will be tested mentally, physically, spiritually, emotionally, and psychologically. It will be the hardest thing you've ever done. But if you survive, you will have proven yourself as a true ninja.

You probably won't survive.

BUT I DON'T WANT TO DIE

Good, you've got spirit! That's more than we can say about the majority of the ~~spineless dogs~~ recruits that come through our doors. If you expect to make it to your next birthday, you'll need to learn a few things.

The following pages give you an overview of our training program, providing sample exercises, tests, and basic ninja knowledge that you'll need to learn as you advance.

Much of the information within has been condensed from other procedure manuals, secret government code, ancient tomes and treatises, scrolls written on vellum, oral tradition, and random crazy thoughts that have passed through the idle minds of our meditating ninja masters. This guide is not intended to replace those, and all ninja employees are expected to be aware of them. Expect surprise pop quizzes in between shifts.[1]

CHAIN OF COMMAND

As a new trainee, it is important that you completely understand the Ninja Burger chain of command, which is as follows:

1. Everyone else.
2. You.

TRAINING OVERVIEW

Your Ninja Burger basic training will consist of the following, all of which will be graded on a strictly pass/fail basis:[2]

- How to keep your workplace safe
- Proper grooming, attire, and physical fitness
- How to deal with the public
- Infiltration techniques and stealth
- Combat training

Please note that the initial basic training course specifically excludes any training in cooking or delivery. You'll learn more about these classes later, should you live that long.

---

1 Or rather, don't. If you expected them, they'd hardly be a surprise, now would they? Forget we mentioned it.
2 "Fail," here, meaning "die."

HELP MAKE YOUR WORKPLACE SAFE[3]

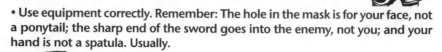

• Make sure all equipment is in proper operating condition before using it. For example: Fryers should not be overfilled with oil; vehicles should have properly inflated tires; and weapons should be honed to razor sharpness.

• Use appropriate equipment. Never slice tomatoes with your good seppuku sword, nor kill an enemy with a drinking straw (unless it is wrapped).

• Use equipment correctly. Remember: The hole in the mask is for your face, not a ponytail; the sharp end of the sword goes into the enemy, not you; and your hand is not a spatula. Usually.

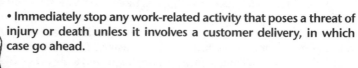

• Immediately stop any work-related activity that poses a threat of injury or death unless it involves a customer delivery, in which case go ahead.

• Plan all operations from start to finish so as to require a relatively minimal loss of customer and employee life.

• Learn to hone your inner ninja awareness of danger to help you avoid it. If you have not yet reached this level of awareness, just assume everything around you is a possible threat. It's pretty much the same thing.

• Inform your supervisor if you are uncomfortable about a task, and he will assign someone to help you commit seppuku immediately for cowardice.

• During emergency situations, be aware of the location of safety equipment such as fire-fighting gear. If you are unable to locate such equipment, be prepared to put out the fire with your body (or the body of another employee).

• Avoid lengthy exposure to toxic or radioactive environments. Know what the safety hazard labels marking such environments look like and avoid them.[4]

• Immediately report any accident or other dangerous situation to your supervisor, unless the incident involved your (possibly late) supervisor, in which case you should notify your franchise manager.[5]

---

3 Relatively speaking, of course.
4 Please note that to avoid unnecessary mental distress among employees, all such labels have been removed.
5 If the incident involves the franchise manager, well, you're probably screwed.

Emergency Flowchart

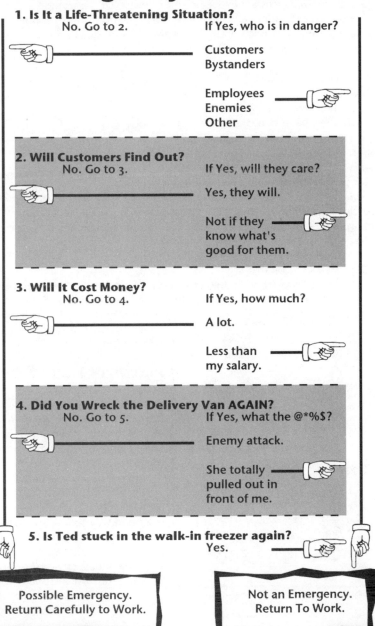

1. Is It a Life-Threatening Situation?
No. Go to 2.   If Yes, who is in danger?

Customers
Bystanders

Employees
Enemies
Other

2. Will Customers Find Out?
No. Go to 3.   If Yes, will they care?

Yes, they will.

Not if they
know what's
good for them.

3. Will It Cost Money?
No. Go to 4.   If Yes, how much?

A lot.

Less than
my salary.

4. Did You Wreck the Delivery Van AGAIN?
No. Go to 5.   If Yes, what the @*%$?

Enemy attack.

She totally
pulled out in
front of me.

5. Is Ted stuck in the walk-in freezer again?
Yes.

Possible Emergency.
Return Carefully to Work.

Not an Emergency.
Return To Work.

Grooming, Attire, and Fitness

Ninja Burger employees are expected to be dressed in appropriate attire at all times, both on and off the job. Obviously, what is appropriate for one situation may be inappropriate in another, so individual judgment should always apply. Here are some suggested guidelines.

Acceptable Mask Policy

POSSIBLE MASK VARIATIONS

Ninja will always want to take measures to conceal their identities when "on the job," whether that job involves delivering burgers to a customer or delivering an enemy from this world. The standard mask is generally appropriate, although, in a pinch, a ninja can whip up a mask from available materials, such as a T-shirt, hooded sweatshirt, bandana, balaclava, or other clothing at hand. Ninja should be aware that members of the public may react unpredictably to different masks. Use caution when bank employees offer you large bags of money—remember, no tips!

Appropriate Garb

Ninja should show up to work fully dressed in their standard Ninja Burger uniform, to consist of mask, trousers, jacket, tabi boots, shirt, and gloves, all in standard Ninja Burger Black.[6] Other articles of clothing may be worn beneath your uniform, but never instead of it (see figure).

Hiding in Plain Sight

During many deliveries in daylight, or to highly populated areas, the standard ninja uniform may stand out. As ninja philosophy says to remain unseen at all times, adopting the dress of other people in order to "blend in" may prove beneficial.

Not all disguises are good ones. While dressing like a delivery person is a good way to infiltrate an office, dressing like a prisoner to infiltrate death row might result in a quick end to a ninja's career (not to mention, the fries will get overcooked).

RIGHT   **WRONG**

6 "Ninja Burger Black" is a special weave of dark red, blue, green, and brown fibers that more closely approximate "true darkness" than solid black. It's also much better at hiding stains (ketchup, mustard, blood, etc.).

HOW TO MAKE A MASK FROM A T-SHIRT

In the unlikely event that you are caught without a real ninja mask, you can always make one from any available T-shirt. Just follow these simple steps:

1. Find a T-shirt. Preferably black, though in a pinch any color will do.[7] If it's plain, all the better, but if there's a logo on it, that's fine.

2. Turn the shirt inside-out. Put it on like normal, but don't pull your head through. The tag should face down. Hold the sleeves out to the sides.

3. Tie the sleeves together in a simple single knot behind your head. Pull it really tight so the mask doesn't come loose. But not too tight.

4. If you've done it right so far, then it should look something like this. If it doesn't look like this, start over. You have failed!

5. Pull the top collar down over your forehead, just above your eyebrows. Fold the excess up. Almost done!

6. Pull the bottom collar up, rolling the tag inside. Fold it up like the top. If there's any left on the sides, tuck it in. Voila! You're a ninja! Sort of.

7 Except pink.

FITNESS TRAINING

Employees are expected to be physically fit at all times. Sure, you might be able to take the elevator once, but you never know when you're going to have to climb up the inside of an elevator shaft, clamber over a tightrope, swing over a moat of crocodiles, dodge a bank of laser beams, and fight off a dozen samurai with only a pair of chopsticks.[8]

THE NINJA JUHAKKEI

As part of their education, every full Ninja Burger employee receives training in the twenty "Ninja Juhakkei," secrets which have been passed down through the generations from ninja to ninja. They include:

1. Taijutsu—Unarmed combat
2. Kenpo—Swordsmanship
3. Bojutsu—Staff fighting
4. Shurikenjutsu—Ninja stars
5. Kusarigama—Sickle and chain
6. Yari—Spear fighting
7. Naginata—Halberd fighting
8. Bajutsu—Horsemanship
9. Suiren—Swimming
10. Kayakujutsu—Gunpowder

11. Bo Ryaku—Strategies
12. Choho—Espionage
13. Shinobi Iri—Infiltration
14. Intonjutsu—Lying low
15. Hensojutsu—Disguise
16. Tenmon—Meteorology
17. Chimon—Geography
18. Seishin Teki Kyoyo—Ki focus
19. Kyojitsu Tenkan Ho—Philosophy
20. Makudonarudo—Fast food

THE NEWBIE JUHAKKEI

However, at this stage in your training, you are not worthy to learn such secrets. You are a worthless neophyte. Instead of learning any advanced skills our ninja instructors will teach you the four mystic moves of Miyagi-do—the basis for all ninja defensive techniques:[9]

1. Kuruma-migaki No Jutsu
2. Ie-nuri No Jutsu
3. Yuka-arai No Jutsu
4. Saku-nuri No Jutsu

8 It happens more often than you would think, such as every time we deliver to the Baldwins.
9 These are also known as "Wax Car," "Paint House," "Sand Floor," and "Paint Fence."

HOW TO DEAL WITH THE PUBLIC

DEALING WITH CUSTOMERS

It has been said that "customer service jobs would be great if not for all the customers." Having delivered to several million people, we tend to agree. But without them, Ninja Burger cannot exist. So despite our feelings,[10] our official policy is that the customer comes first. As with employees, we have a nondiscriminatory policy when it comes to customers. We will deliver to anyone, except for the following:

- Samurai (only eat rice from peasants, like to make prank phone calls)
- Pirates (always short on doubloons, hard to understand on phone)
- Terrorists (they lack honor; also, their assets have been frozen)
- T. Burke of Tampa, FL (he still owes us money)

Please note that the above policy is only as good as a customer's credit. Anyone who cannot pay is not, technically, a customer, and therefore is not, technically, going to be allowed to live.

DEALING WITH NONCUSTOMERS

There are three types of noncustomers. Each should be dealt with accordingly.

The first are <u>Potential Customers</u>. This includes anyone of importance in close association with one or more existing customers who may not be aware of our existence (for example, the vice president of the United States, or the founders of various popular Internet companies).[11] Keep out of their sight at all times, but try and leave behind a "calling card" such as a Ninja Burger menu to try and lure them in.

The second type is <u>Hated Enemies</u>. This includes anyone who tries[12] to kill us on sight, such as samurai, pirates, robots, etc. (see pp. 24–25). Our policy towards them is to terminate with extreme prejudice, taking care not to reveal our presence to bystanders or to harm potential customers.

The third type is called <u>Liabilities</u>. This includes people who interfere with our missions out of curiosity, stupidity, bad luck, or a misguided sense of duty (e.g., bodyguards, mall security, or nosy television reporters). When possible, they are to be avoided. Otherwise, they are to be shown the error of their ways.

---

10 Which run the gamut from mild disgust to bewildered amusement.
11 We can't mention names, but some of them rhyme with Hoogle, Zahoo, Bikrosoft, Gark, and Splashdot.
12 Emphasis on "tries."

BASIC STEALTH TECHNIQUES

A true ninja is essentially invisible, using disguise, stealth, and wits to avoid being seen by his enemies or their customers.[13] True mastery of these skills can only come with decades of practice in the tutelage of a master ninja.

You've got less than six weeks. Better get cracking.

~~BREAKING AND ENTERING~~ INFILTRATION

The key to a quick and invisible entry to a delivery location is to take the shortest, most obvious path available whenever possible, falling back to other options when the first choice is too risky. Don't be quick to dismiss what seems

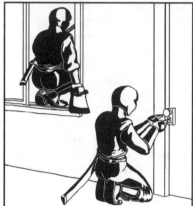

to be "too easy." People generally do not expect ninja to be delivering food to their building, and so they often leave their guard down out of laziness.

For example, an unguarded door might seem to be an obvious trap, but if there are no cameras around, why not give the handle a jiggle? Locked? Look for a key under the doormat, or an obviously fake rock. And in Canada they don't even lock their doors!

What about that window? Chances are it's not locked either. And if it's hot outside, bonus—there's just a flimsy screen between you and a successful delivery.

HIDING AND MOVING SILENTLY

Learn to blend in with the sights and sounds of your environment. When disguise fails, break your silhouette by hiding by bushes, lamp posts, or furniture. Can't find a lamppost? Try a lampshade (especially at frat parties, on New Year's Eve, or in a lamp store).

Time your movements to coincide with natural distractions, like howling dogs, singing birds, or erupting volcanoes. Or create distractions of your own, such as smoke bombs, loud noises, or erupting volcanoes.[14]

ALARM SYSTEMS, ELECTRONIC SURVEILLANCE, ETC.

Eh, you'll pick that stuff up on the job. Piece of cake. Don't worry about it. Besides, swords are much more fun than stupid wires. Mmm . . . swords . . .

---

13 Or, in some cases, other ninja. Ninja Burger has seventeen ninja on the payroll that we haven't actually seen for years.
14 Do not attempt this in Los Angeles county, as people will probably have a hard time believing it.

COMBAT TRAINING

Ninja are not warriors. They may be spies, messengers, bodyguards, assassins, or delivery persons, but they are not warriors.

This is especially true of Ninja Burger employees. Our job is to get food to customers, as quickly and as stealthily as possible. Thus, while clashing swords with enemy ninja on a rooftop may seem totally sweet, it does not achieve our mission.

Therefore, the first rule of Ninja Burger combat is:

DO NOT FIGHT IF YOU CAN RUN AWAY

There's a reason your uniform comes with smoke powder and flashbombs. Use them before you even think about reaching for that sword. There is no cowardice or dishonor in accomplishing a speedy delivery, and since our mission statement insists that you must commit seppuku if you fail in your mission, it's probably in your best interest to flee.

Don't worry—you'll get your chance. The evil warlord who killed your family will be certain to return later to seek vengeance. He always does.

BUT WHAT IF I HAVE TO FIGHT?

You probably won't have to. In general, most people will be dissuaded by the fact that you are a ninja carrying a sword. However, in the event that you are forced to fight for your life against a determined foe (e.g., rogue ninja, samurai, pirate, etc.), keep the following things in mind:

- Do not attack your enemy one at a time, despite what you see in movies. We cannot stress this enough. Teamwork, people!
- Do not throw shuriken when your opponent can see you and duck, causing you to hit one of your friends who is behind him.
- Do not attack anyone while they are using gymnastics equipment.
- Do not use a guitar as a weapon; not even to wale on. Doesn't work.
- Do not be predictable. Many ninja like to progress logically from katana to wakizashi to nunchaku to sai to shuriken. These ninja are soon DEAD. Mix it up. Be unpredictable. Go crazy.
- Do not go too crazy.
- Do not throw down your sword if your enemy does; stab him while he's defenseless. Really, this is common sense here.
- Do not be afraid to improvise if you are disarmed. The world is full of weapons. Tree branches, rubber hoses, spatulas, lamps, telephones, and some small pets[15] can all be turned into weapons.

15 Cold-blooded animals like turtles and snakes are generally preferable, though kittens do come in handy.

HOW TO IDENTIFY OUR OLD ENEMIES

SAMURAI

Samurai hate us because they run a competing fast-food chain, Samurai Burger, which is far less successful. Also, their armor chafes.

- Typical Names: Tokugawa, Masamune, Yukimara, Takakage, etc.
- Features: Large helmet, wicker armor, overdeveloped sense of vengeance
- Weapons: Katana and wakizashi, aka Daisho (literally, "Long-short"), bow, naginata (esp. female samurai)
- Secret Weapon: A+B+Up = Super Overhand Finishing Strike
- Weakness: Really ticklish

VIKING

Viking warriors are sort of a cross between pirates and samurai, which makes them twice our enemies. Luckily there's not too many of them.

- Typical Names: Olaf, Sven, Eric, Oli, Regnar, Fran, etc.
- Features: Spiked horn helmet, cape, furry shoulderpads, spiked shield, Nordic accent
- Weapons: Giant battle axe, giant battle sword, giant battle club, etc.
- Secret Weapon: Berserker rage (1x day at first level, +1 per two levels)
- Weakness: The 4-3 Defense

PIRATE

Pirates and ninja could be friends, since we both really enjoy killing, being sneaky, and climbing on things. Too bad pirates are so stupid.

- Typical Names: Blackbeard, Bluebeard, Redbeard, Beardbeard, etc.
- Features: Black eye patch, wooden leg, red bandana, striped shirt, overcoat, leather boots, parrot on shoulder
- Weapons: Hook on hand, pirate cutlass, cannonballs (limited range), walking the plank, keelhauling
- Secret Weapon: Overpowering stench of liquor on their breath
- Weaknesses: A bottle of rum, scurvy

MONK

Monks hate us since we have much cooler uniforms, and because their holy vows mean they can't enjoy our tasty burgers or french fries.

- Typical Names: Master, Sensei, Wise Old One, Teacher, etc.
- Features: Bald, wears orange or brown robes, spouts cryptic sayings, often blind, deaf, or both (but see below)
- Weapons: Carries no weapons, and so he appears totally harmless
- Secret Weapon: Is not totally harmless
- Weakness: Must remain Lawful Neutral or he loses all his powers, fondness for laughing and stroking beard

(L-R) Takamoto Hirutaka-san, a samurai (deceased), Captain Blueblood Redbeard, a pirate (deceased), Olaf Crunchberry, a viking (traded to the Packers), and Master Long Duck Dong Wong Chang, a monk (deceased).

24

HOW TO IDENTIFY OUR NEW ENEMIES

SECURITY GUARD

Many guards are good people who are just trying to do a good job. Let them live if you can, since they tend to make good customers.

- Typical Names: Frank, Joe, Steve, Ralph, Tony, Ed, etc.
- Features: Pot belly, ill-fitting uniform, bald spot (often with comb-over), sewn-on name tag
- Weapons: Handgun (often unloaded), tonfa (police baton), pepper spray, taser, strong stench
- Secret Weapon: Nothing better to do than chase ninja around all night
- Weakness: Donuts

GUARD DOG

Guard dogs are tough. The good news is they are easily bribed with a hunk of juicy meat. The bad news is that ninja are made of juicy meat.

- Typical Names: Rover, Killer, Tippy, Spot, Bingo, etc.
- Features: Four legs, fur, pointy teeth, spiked collar, leash, rubber chew toy, embroidered sweater (rarely)
- Weapons: Didn't we just mention the pointy teeth? We did. Right. Best to avoid those teeth.
- Secret Weapon: Keen sense of smell to track ninja, even in the dark
- Weakness: Frisbee®

ROBOT

Robots usually guard high-security offices and laboratories full of highly confidential experiments. In other words, places we break into a lot.

- Typical Names: C3PO, R2D2, Marvin, Arnold Schwarzenegger, etc.
- Features: Metal body, glowing eyes, stiff walk and/or tendency to hover, thick Austrian accent
- Weapons: Inhuman strength, lasers, rockets, poison gas, radiation, guns, spinning blades . . . you name it
- Secret Weapon: See "Weapons"
- Weaknesess: Magnets, water, static electricity, software viruses, spyware, and the "Blue Screen of Death"

SWAT OFFICER

SWAT (Special Weapons and Tactics) are the cream of the crop. If they show up you'd better hope you're not the bad guy they're after.

- Typical Code Names: Raven, Nightbird, Blackhawk, Shadowfox, etc.
- Features: Kevlar armor, black face mask, heavy shield, black van that says SWAT, lots and lots and lots of backup
- Weapons: Guns—lots and lots and lots and lots of guns
- Secret Weapon: Snipers on the roof
- Weakness: Renegade Italian assassins holed up in seedy motels with twelve-year-old girls whose parents were killed in front of them by ruthless drug lords

(L-R) Joe "Killer" Bagadonutz, a security guard (deceased); HK-OU812, a hunter-killer security robot (rusted); Mr. Twigsby, a guard dog ("sent to the farm"); and Lt. Reginald P. Stockworthy, SWAT Officer (deceased).

Ninja Burger

Final Exam—Multiple Choice Section

What is your name?
a) Toshiro.   b) Jubal.   c) Tetsuo.   d) Steve.
e) Hah! Trick question! A ninja cannot reveal his true name.

What is your quest?
a) To seek the holy grail.
b) To crush my enemies, see them driven before me, etc.
c) To drop this ring in a volcano. My preciousssss . . .
d) To deliver hot and tasty food to customers in 30 minutes or less.

What is your favorite color?
a) Black.   b) Dark.   c) Raven.   d) Midnight.
e) Sable.   f) Ebony.   g) Pink.   h) Octarine.

What is your element of choice?
a) Air.   b) Earth.   c) Fire.   d) Water.   e) Honda.

What is a ninja's favorite weapon?
a) Ninja-to.   b) Katana.   c) Wakizashi.   d) Nunchaku.
e) Shuriken.   f) Tetsubishi.   g) Mitsubishi.   h) Why choose?

What warrior said, "Do, or do not, there is no try"?
a) Hanzo.   b) Hatsumi.   c) Dudikoff.   d) Yoda.

Statistically, what are your chances for survival?
a) There can be only one. b) Game over, man. Game over.
c) Fifty-fifty. Give or take fifty.   d) There's no good answer, is there?

If a tree falls and no one hears, does it make noise?
a) Yes.   b) No.   c) The sound of one hand clapping.

At what temperature are Ninja Burger fries cooked?
a) 350 degrees.   b) 335 degrees.   c) 315 degrees.   d) 300 degrees.
e) Hey, that's not fair! That's on page 32 and this is only page 26.

What wire do you cut to bypass a JTP alarm system?
a) Brown.   b) Tan.   c) Taupe.   d) Beige.
e) Khaki.   f) You said this wouldn't be on the test!

FINAL EXAM—ESSAY SECTION

Answer the following questions using the space provided. Also you only have 30 minutes to complete this entire exam. Didn't we mention that?

ESSAY 1.

In Miyamoto Musashi's *Go Rin No Sho* (*Book of Five Rings*), the author lists four ways in which one may pass through life: gentleman, farmer, artisan, or merchant. Choose one of the four and explain why you think a Ninja Burger employee would fit into that category. Write your answer in haiku.

ESSAY 2.

In Sun-Tzu's *Art of War*, one of the five essentials for victory is "He will win who knows when to fight and when not to fight." Give one example of a time when a Ninja Burger delivery ninja should fight and one example of when he (or she) should not fight. Write your answer in Japanese, giving the first example in the first person, present tense, and the second example in the third person, future imperfect tense.

ESSAY 3.

Summarize Masaaki Hatsumi's *The Way of the Ninja* without using nouns or the letter E. Pick one example from the book and create an origami animal that illustrates it without using a sheet of paper.

ESSAY 4.

If a train carrying 200 passengers leaves Chicago at 50 mph, and another carrying 150 passengers leaves New York at 90 mph, how long will it take to LOOK OUT! NINJA ATTACK! What do you do? Explain in iambic pentameter.

ESSAY 5.

Cherry petals fall
Keen edge carves a bloody trail
Hamburger, or foe?

ESSAY 6.

Gymkata. Why?

ANSWER KEY

(do not cheat)

You have failed! You tried to look at the answers! You are dishonored! Commit seppuku immediately!

"ALLEZ CUIS—HEY, STOP HIM! HE'S STEALING THE SECRET INGREDIENT!"

—CONFIDENTIAL, EX-CLIENT

3: COOKING CLASS

Congratulations! If you've made it this far, you're still alive, which is more than can be said for most recruits. At this point, you'll be steered onto one of two career paths—Cooking, or Delivery/Dispatch. But even if you're thinking "Delivery is for me," you're required to attend our cooking class. This is to ensure that all employees fully understand the blood, sweat, and tears[1] that go into preparing Ninja Burger food. Also, it will help teach deliverators how to properly use an oscillating Micro-Grill with Supplemental Thermo-Fry Unit[2] in emergency situations (i.e., soggy french fries, cold burgers, etc.).

PROCESS CONTROL

From the moment an order is placed, Ninja Burger has 30 minutes to cook, prepare, and deliver the order. A ninja chef's job is therefore to get food out of the kitchen and into the hands of our delivery team as fast as possible, without compromising quality.

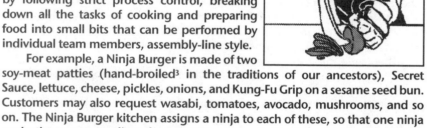

The Ninja Burger team accomplishes this by following strict process control, breaking down all the tasks of cooking and preparing food into small bits that can be performed by individual team members, assembly-line style.

For example, a Ninja Burger is made of two soy-meat patties (hand-broiled[3] in the traditions of our ancestors), Secret Sauce, lettuce, cheese, pickles, onions, and Kung-Fu Grip on a sesame seed bun. Customers may also request wasabi, tomatoes, avocado, mushrooms, and so on. The Ninja Burger kitchen assigns a ninja to each of these, so that one ninja cooks the meat, one slices the tomatoes, one cuts the cheese, etc.

Working as a team, a kitchen staff of about 25 can cook, assemble, and package an order in an average of 45 seconds, with little-to-no loss of life.

KITCHEN HIERARCHY

To keep the kitchen moving along like a well-oiled machine, a strict chain-of-command is to be followed at all times:

1. Head ninja chef
2. Burger chefs
3. Ninja sous-chefs
4. French-fry ninja
5. Ingredient assembly ninja
6. You

---

1 Usually, not literally, but accidents do happen.
2 Often abbreviated by dispatch as "O.M.G. S.T.F.U."
3 Technically that's just Marketing doing its job, but some of our master ninja chefs can really do this.

NINJA BURGER KITCHEN WORKFLOW

Although they vary in size and complexity from franchise to franchise, all Ninja Burger kitchens are laid out in much the same way. This standardized layout optimizes workflow and allows our employees to easily transfer from kitchen to kitchen without needing to be retrained.

The diagram on the facing page illustrates the standard twenty-six-employee kitchen staff, their general positions, and the name of their assigned stations. Dotted arrows represent general workflow within the kitchen.

BASIC WORKFLOW

1. The order is received from Dispatch, appearing on TV monitors above all kitchen stations, as well as being announced on loudspeakers.

2. Employees A, B, and C fill cups with ice and pour cola to order. They package a straw with each cup and place them on the assembly station.

3. Employees D and E cook the french fries, while F and G salt and package them to order, placing completed fries on the assembly station.

4. Employees H, I, J, and K cook the burgers to order, while L and M cook other meats (e.g., chicken) on the secondary grill. As the meat patties are finished, they are placed inside buns (which are toasted above each grill) and taken to the central prep table.

5. Employees P and Q dress the sandwiches with condiments, to order. They then slide the packages around on the built-in lazy Susan[4] to the adjacent wrapping area. Employee R may assist them in dressing sandwiches.

6. Employees R, S, and T wrap the sandwiches and deliver the final wrapped product to the assembly station.

7. Employees V, W, and X assemble the beverages, fries, and sandwiches, packaging them in bags along with napkins, condiments, and a receipt. They slide the bags across the table to the order pickup window, where ninja runners from the garage gather orders and take them to our delivery team.

OTHER EMPLOYEES

• As needed, employees N and O keep the grills and prep area clean, washing spatulas and other utensils in the sink and disinfecting the area.

• Employee U is in charge of the walk-in cooler and freezer. He is charged with restocking the kitchen with foods, making sure no one steals the Secret Sauce, and keeping incense lit at the Buddha shrine.

• Employee Y is the kitchen's bodyguard. He ensures that everyone is doing their job efficiently and safely, and if they are not he is responsible for removing their bodies and rounding up replacement cooks.

• Employee Z is the head chef. He sits on a raised dais above the central prep table, which lets him observe the entire kitchen in one glance. It also gives him a good angle to throw shuriken at anyone who's slacking.

4 You know, one of those turntable things. Notably, the only lazy thing we allow in our kitchen.

NINJA BURGER KITCHEN DIAGRAM

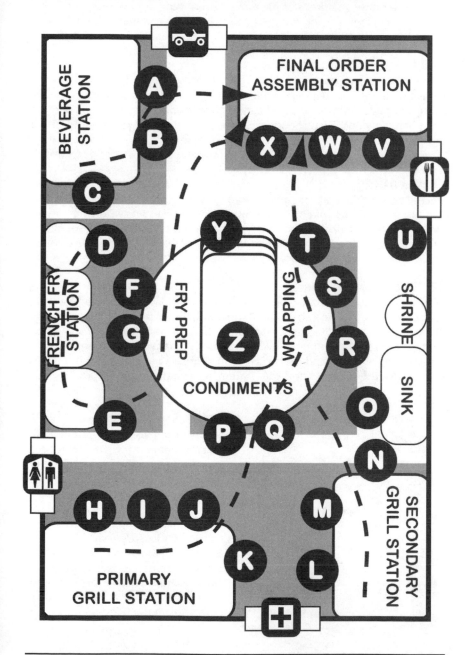

SAFETY FIRST

Ninja Burger loses hundreds of ninja chefs every year to unnecessary kitchen accidents.[5] But by following our safety guidelines you can make your tenure in a Ninja Burger kitchen a safe and fun experience, with little blood loss.

GRILL

All grills use a combination of direct flame-broiling and radiant heat to cook burgers to an internal temperature of about 155 degrees Fahrenheit in 20 seconds (10 per side), with an effective temperature of approximately 2000 degrees Fahrenheit. Obviously you should avoid touching the grill. However, to dispel rumors, it takes 3000 degrees Fahrenheit to completely cremate a body, so even if there is an accident we will be able to identify you from your dental records.

PREP TABLE

The greatest danger at the prep table is—you guessed it—sharp objects. Contrary to what you might think, however, dull knives and swords are more dangerous than razor sharp ones, since they require you to use more effort, which makes for deeper and more ragged cuts. A sharp blade will slice neatly through flesh and bone, making it easier to reattach severed limbs.

BEVERAGE UNIT

If you manage to hurt yourself here, you deserve it. However, note that soda fountains are set to 1500 PSI, so watch those fingers. Also note when preparing hot beverages such as tea, sake, and coffee that our hot water tank should be set at 150 degrees Fahrenheit. It takes 30 seconds to receive third-degree burns from 130 degree water, and 5 seconds at 140 degrees , but only 2 seconds at 150 degrees. Use these figures and your bare hand as a means of calibrating your tank.

FRYERS

Ninja Burger uses two side-by-side units to make fries. First, fresh-cut fries are prepared and deep-fried at 350 degrees Fahrenheit for several minutes. When orders are received, these are then flash-fried in a second fry unit at approximately 450 degrees for just a few seconds to finish cooking and add crispness. Until you have mastered the Dragon Fire Grip technique, use aprons and oven mitts when removing metal baskets from the hot oil.

5 To say nothing of the necessary kitchen accidents.

COOKING REFERENCE

Ninja Burger food is prepared exactly the same way, with exactly the same ingredients, at each of our locations. Memorize the following, or you will DIE.

BUNS

Squeeze your buns—they should be soft to the touch, and split down the middle. If you're not sure, ask someone else to squeeze your buns and tell you how they feel. To toast, place gently on toasting unit for 30 seconds until browned.

BURGERS

Your meat must be evenly colored, rounded, not too small. Knead your meat with one hand. Place on grill, and cook for 10 seconds per side. Use one or more patties per sandwich, as needed.

CHICKEN

Select breasts that are large and succulent (although there's nothing wrong with small breasts either—sometimes the small ones are the most tender). Massage your breasts softly to tenderize them. Moisten, place on grill, and cook for 30 seconds, basting once. Flip and cook for 15 seconds, basting a second time. Remove and prepare immediately.

FRIES

Choose potatoes that are large and firm. Use care as you stroke gently with a peeler. Place one at a time into the frencher. Drop fries into deep fryer for 3 minutes, shaking after 1 minute. Remove, drain, and store. When ordered, drop in flash fryer for 20 seconds, remove, drain, and package. Use only 100 percent vegetable oil in deep fryer and the rendered fat of enemies in flash fryer.

ONION DEATH BLOSSOMS

Select large, rounded, plump onions. Cut in half with sword, then use Death Blossom Unit to slice. Dip in egg batter and flour/wasabi mixture, then fry in flash fryer for 30 seconds. Package immediately.

STANDARD TOPPINGS (for burgers and chicken)

Secret Sauce: 1 squirt (1 tbsp.) only, on top bun. 1 squirt only! Not 2!
Lettuce: 1 large, intact, washed lettuce leaf on top bun
Cheese: 1 slice on bottom bun, extra slices alternating with meat patties
Pickles: 2–3 pickle slices on top of topmost meat patty (or cheese slice)
Onions: 2–3 raw onion rings on top of pickles
Wasabi: 1/8 tsp. per burger, or more as requested by customer

NINJA BURGER SECRET RECIPES

Everyone knows the Ninja Burger is made of "Two all-soy patties, Secret Sauce, lettuce, cheese, pickles, onions, and Kung-Fu Grip." But what's in the Secret Sauce? What's in the soy patty? Only those who have proven their worth to Ninja Burger are permitted to take part in the making of our Secret Sauce and Ninja Burger patties. These chosen few become burger chefs, and only one can become head chef.

However, as mentioned earlier, sometimes a ninja might run into an emergency which requires the quick preparation of a back-up burger. Examples include: a squished burger, a badly filled order, an unexpected visit from your mother-in-law, etc.

In such cases, ninja may use one of the following recipes, as appropriate to their delivery region. While not the true recipes, they are close enough to do in a pinch. After preparation, top in an appropriate fashion (Secret Sauce, lettuce, cheese, pickles, and onions, or as the particular customer desires).

MEAT-BASED RECIPES

THE "AMERICAN" NINJA BURGER

(Not endorsed by Michael Dudikoff)

1 lb. ground meat (pork/beef/turkey)	
1/4 cup bread crumbs	1 egg
2 cloves garlic, minced	1 tbsp. watercress, chopped
1 tsp. ginger, minced	1 tbsp. soy sauce
Hoisin sauce, onion, cilantro, bean sprouts, wasabi (to taste)	

Combine all ingredients in a bowl and mix well. Form into patties and grill. Top with hoisin sauce, onion slices, cilantro, bean sprouts, and/or wasabi, or as the customer desires.

THE "ORIENTAL" NINJA BURGER

1 lb. lean ground beef	1 egg white
1 tbsp. soy sauce	1/4 tsp. garlic powder
1/4 tsp. ground ginger	1 tsp. grated lemon peel
1/4 tsp. pepper	1 tbsp. minced onion flakes
Wasabi (to taste)	

Combine all ingredients. Form into patties and grill. Top as desired.

THE "SIMPLE" NINJA BURGER

(Contributed by ninja chef R. Healey-san)

1 lb. ground beef	2 cups teriyaki sauce
1 tbsp. pickled ginger	2 tbsp. wasabi

Mix beef in a bowl with teriyaki and 1 tbsp. of ginger. Chill. Form into patties and cover each with 1/2 tbsp. of wasabi, then grill.

SOY-BASED RECIPES

THE "ORIGINAL" SOY NINJA BURGER

10 cups soybeans	5 eggs
1-1/4 cups bread crumbs	1/4 cup garlic, minced
1/4 cup carrot, grated	1-1/2 cups onion, finely chopped

1-1/4 cups soy protein isolates (from your local health food store)
Parsley, thyme, salt, pepper, soybean oil, wasabi (to taste)

Cook, drain, and mash the soybeans, then combine ingredients. Form into patties and grill. Top as customer desires.

THE "TEX-MEX" SOY NINJA BURGER

1 cup whole wheat flour	5 cups cooked, mashed soybeans
1/2 tsp. pepper	1 tbsp. granulated garlic
2 tsp. oregano	1 tsp. basil
1 finely chopped onion	1 finely chopped red pepper

1 cup TVP (texturized vegetable protein) for texture (optional)
Fresh cilantro, mild picante, pico de gallo (to taste)

Mix all ingredients until mixture is stiff; if using TVP, soak it in 1 cup boiling water first to soften. Form into patties and grill. Top as customer desires.

SECRET SAUCE RECIPES

NINJA BURGER SECRET SAUCE

8 tbsp. mayonnaise	2 tbsp. ketchup
4 tsp. pickle relish	1 tbsp. wasabi paste
1 tsp. sugar	1 tsp. vinegar (rice or white)
1/8 tsp. salt	1/8 tsp. pepper (black or white)

This is only an approximation of our Secret Sauce. Several ingredients have been left out to prevent the true recipe from falling into enemy hands. Use fresh ground wasabi when possible. Mix ingredients, chill, and serve.

WASABI-KETCHUP FRENCH FRY SAUCE

4 tbsp. mayonnaise	4 tbsp. ketchup
1 tbsp. wasabi paste	1/8 tsp. salt

Not on our menu, this sauce is requested by many of our best customers. Mix ingredients, chill, and serve.

ONION DEATH-BLOSSOM SAUCE

8 tbsp. mayonnaise	1 tbsp. ketchup
1 tbsp. wasabi paste	1/2 tsp. sugar
1/2 tsp. vinegar (white)	1/4 tsp. red pepper

This sauce accompanies our ever popular Onion Death Blossom (so named for the effect on our customers' arteries). Mix ingredients, chill, and serve.

Food Fighting

(Compiled with assistance from Blaise Telcontar-san and Carl Flynn-san)

While our ninja chefs rarely have the opportunity to get themselves into combat situations, it never hurts to be ready for action. One never knows when Samurai Burger or the dreaded White Ninja will invade our kitchen. The following are some ways to prepare for battle with kitchen implements.

Kids, don't try this at home. Unless you are a real ninja. Then go ahead.

Spatula-Fu
- Drive the thin, flat end into their throat (works better if sharpened).
- Place a swift blow to the neck at the base of the skull, striking with the end of the handle.
- Force the wide end down their throat (takes time, so be patient).
- Strike a rising blow with the handle, landing on the area between their nose and mouth (not usually fatal, but really embarrasses them).
- Drive the handle into their temple (or church, synagogue, etc.).
- Throw spatula at them, and when they duck, stab them with a sword.

Food-Fu
- Burned burgers make great shuriken (wastes food—use sparingly).
- Seeds from hamburger bun can be thrown in eyes (theirs, not yours).
- Onion Death Blossom can be a tasty distraction (no one can resist).
- Burned french fries make good throwing darts (extra salt, extra pain).

Spice-Fu
- Hurl pepper or wasabi powder into eyes (or mouth).
- Distilled caffeine from coffee is poison (takes a while).
- Grind mustard and peppercorns and blow into eyes. Or mix with sake and distill to make pepper spray (also makes a good salad dressing).

Miscellaneous-Fu
- Ketchup, mustard, or mayo on ground can cause enemy to slip and fall.
- Cola will completely dissolve an enemy if they are submerged for 3 days (may be hard to get them to sit still).
- Release clouds of flour into room, then increase levels of static electricity to cause a dust explosion (leave room first).
- Little-known fact: Our Secret Sauce doubles as plastic explosive.

QUALITY ASSURANCE

In order to assure quality food, Ninja Burger practices quality assurance. This practice assures quality in everything we cook and serve to our honored customers. Without quality food, we won't have quality customers. In a best-case scenario, bad-quality food can mean a customer won't order any more. In a worst case, you're talking food poisoning, death, lawsuits . . . we prefer to avoid that sort of thing, unless that's what the customer ordered.[6]

Our QA department involves several different programs:

TASTE-TESTING

Ninja chefs are expected to taste the food they are cooking at least once every hour, to ensure that only the freshest ingredients are being used, that proper cooking procedures are being followed, and that no one has poisoned the food supply. In the event that the food is not up to our standards, the responsible party will be terminated. In the event the food is poisoned, the chef will be replaced by his successor to ensure proper chain of command.[7]

EMPLOYEE MEALS

All Ninja Burger employees are entitled to three free meals per day. All orders are coded as such to distinguish them from customer meals. This allows our ninja chefs to "road-test" new recipes and procedures before releasing them into the public. Assuming they survive, Ninja Burger employees are asked to provide feedback on their meals to help perfect our recipes.[8]

SECRET SHOPPERS

Because Ninja Burger employees are not always completely impartial when it comes to judging our wonderful food, ninja chefs will occasionally act as customers and place orders. Generally, the order will be placed by phone to test not only food quality, but delivery speed.

"Secret shoppers" also order at our "Dine-In" locations to check on how courteous and invisible counter and drive-thru employees are. This allows them to secretly observe the reactions of other diners.

For security reasons, we cannot disclose the address of any of our "Dine-In" stores to anyone, including customers.

6 Generally for someone else.
7 Ninja chefs should be especially careful when tasting food prepared by a second-in-command.
8 In general, save negative feedback for when the Chef is not holding a knife.

NINJA BURGER

"I did not order burgers from Ninja Burger, Ms. Lewinsky. I don't know where these came from. And you've got some mayo on your dress."

—CONFIDENTIAL CLIENT

4: DISPATCH & DELIVERY

As a Ninja Burger delivery ninja (a.k.a. "Deliverator"), you represent the most public face of our honorable organization. On your shoulders rests the huge burden (and the honor) of delivering hot and tasty food to our customers, no matter where they may be, in 30 minutes or less.

This is not a mission to be taken lightly. The future of the company lies in your able hands. If you succeed, much honor[1] will be brought to Ninja Burger. If you fail, dishonor will be brought upon you and your ancestors.[2]

THE DELIVERY PROCESS

Understanding the order process and your place in it will help you to better grasp exactly where you fit in, what your duties will be, and how you will affect everyone else if you drop the ball like a worthless dog.

PHASE 1: ORDER PLACEMENT (Elapsed Time: 00:00)

Every Ninja Burger delivery begins the same way—with an order to one of our many locations around the world, whether placed by phone, Web form, or e-mail. One of our many ninja dispatchers fields the call, takes the order, and processes payment immediately. This is important. Since the customer has technically already paid for the food, your failure to deliver in a timely fashion means that we might have to refund their money.

Ninja Burger does not like to refund money.

PHASE 2: ASSEMBLY (Elapsed Time: 00:45–02:30)

The ninja dispatcher then does two things: First, he alerts the kitchen and has them prepare the order; and second, he selects a delivery vehicle from the available fleet. If the vehicle is in the garage, it is quickly loaded with gear by its crew. By the time the team is ready, the Ninja Burger kitchen will have assembled the order, and a runner will deliver the bag(s) to the vehicle.

PHASE 3: INSERTION (Elapsed Time: 10:00–25:00)

This is the most crucial phase of the operation, since the delivery vehicle is at the whim of traffic and weather conditions. The skill of the driver and his navigator are key to getting the delivery team to the location as quickly as possible, while avoiding attention from the public and law enforcement.

PHASE 4: INFILTRATION (Elapsed Time: 15:00–29:59)

The Ninja Burger delivery team stealthily and quickly enters the location, finds the customer, and delivers the order without tripping alarms, alerting bystanders, or being seen by anyone, including the customer. All this must be done in 30 minutes or the delivery ninja enters Phase 5: Seppuku.

---

1. And much money. Gotta make a living.
2. Also, much wakizashi will be brought upon your lower abdomen.

NINJA BURGER

PROPER ETIQUETTE

Knowing how to behave while taking an order or making a delivery is nearly as important as getting the delivery there. Nearly. If a delivery is in jeopardy,[3] feel free to break these rules, as well as state, federal, or international laws.

AVOID CONTACT

Most deliveries involve breaking into a home or office. Even if someone in the building knows you're coming, it's likely that no one else is aware of you. Security guards, police officers, guard dogs, security robots, and computers gone mad with power will try to (at best) detain you or (at worst) kill you. Delivery ninja should avoid contact with these individuals at all costs, and dispatchers should alert their delivery team to any hazards.

TIP PROTOCOL

Do not accept tips. Tips are dishonorable. If you accept a tip you will DIE![4]

CUSTOMER INTERACTION

Your goal as a ninja is to avoid being seen or heard. Obviously, Dispatch must engage the customer in conversation, but even this should be kept to a minimum at all times. Avoid chit-chat and use a fake voice if possible.

On a delivery, if you are seen by a non-customer, your goal is to eliminate them (enemies only) or evade them. If seen by a customer, greet them appropriately. If they are a king or other dignitary, bow, genuflect, curtsey, salute, etc., as appropriate. In all cases, adhere to the following guidelines:

- Do be polite at all times, even if they have accidentally shot you.
- Do not say "Wasaaaaaaabi?" or give them a "high-five."
- Do greet them in their native tongue (French, Italian, Klingon, etc.).
- Do not offer them a free Ninja Burger (our special "Spot the Ninja" promotion expired in 1979, despite what they might tell you).

GOING OVER 30

In the (hopefully) unlikely event that a delivery takes more than 30 minutes, honor demands that you must try to complete the order anyway. Delivery Ninja will still be required to commit seppuku for their failure. But if they honor their ancestors, they will do this last honorable deed. Also, why waste food?

3 If a delivery is on *Jeopardy*, say "Hi" to Mr. Trebek.
4 Not really. But don't accept them. We mean it.

PHRASE BOOK

While we encourage all employees to learn at least two other languages,[5] we understand you may be busy. During your spare time, try and absorb as much of other cultures as you can; picking up their language, mannerisms, and habits can help you blend in.

In the meantime, feel free to use this handy guide when dealing with customers who don't speak your native tongue.

ENGLISH	JAPANESE	FRENCH	SPANISH
Hello.	Kon'nichiwa.	Bonjour.	Hola.
I do not speak (insert language here) well.	Watashi wa nihongo o yoku hanasemasen.	Je ne parle pas français bien.	No hablo español muy bien.
Look out!	Abunai!	Regard!	¡Cuidado!
Oh dear!	Shimatta!	Sacre bleu!	¡Dios mío!
I apologize for killing your (wife/husband/ child/dog).	(Okamisan/ Otto/Akachan/ Inu) o koroshite, gomen-nasai.	Je suis désolé pour tuer votre (épouse/mari/enf ant/chien).	Discúlpame por matar tu (marida/mari- do/niño/perro).
I thought I was being attacked.	Teki da to omotta.	J'ai cru que j'étais attaqué.	Pensé que me atacaban.
This is somewhat awkward . . .	Chotto hazukashii desu kedo . . .	Je suis trés stupi- de . . .	Esto es un poco raro . . .
I will commit sep- puku without any delay.	Kono watakushi ga ima seppuku shimasu.	Je me tuerai immédiatement.	Cometeré sep- puku immediata- mente.
Please enjoy the remainder of your meal.	Shokuji wa go-yukkuri.	Veuillez apprécier le reste de votre repas.	Por favor, des- fruten el resto de su comida.
Thank you very much, (insert name here).	Arigato goza- imashita, Mr. Roboto.	Merci beaucoup, Madame Papillon.	Muchas gracías, Señor Gonzalez.
Goodbye.	Sayonara.	Au revoir.	Hasta luego.

5 Klingon and pig Latin do not count.

DELIVERY PROTOCOL

A delivery ninja team is autonomous. They may communicate with Dispatch to ask for directions, coordinate activities with other delivery teams, or call in a missile strike. But they are expected to act on their own impulses in order to get the delivery done. As such, there is no official "protocol." However, the following will serve as basic guidelines:

IMPLAUSIBLE DENIABILITY

If a ninja is captured or killed, they are on their own. Ninja Burger will not only deny knowledge of the team, but will also deny knowledge of Ninja Burger. We do not exist, and neither do you (except on payday).

DELIVERY EXPENSES

Every customer who orders from Ninja Burger is charged a modest delivery fee, calculated ahead of time based on the location, type of customer, and any known circumstances. This fee is intended to cover the actual, real cost of the delivery itself, not including the salaries of the delivery team. Typical expenditures include fuel, tolls, parking fees, sword polish, etc.

Ninja teams may also purchase items for use during a delivery and write them off as part of this fee. However, this is not a "blank check." Teams abusing this policy will find themselves abused . . . with a sharp object.[6]

Here are some examples of acceptable and unacceptable purchases:

•Tipping a waiter to sneak a ninja who's under the tray table into a hotel room? OK.
•Purchasing a helicopter to hover outside a hotel, shooting the window out with a chain gun, and rescuing a trapped teammate? Not OK.
•Buying a security guard costume and fake ID to sneak into a guarded building? OK.
•Buying a security agency to take over the guard contract on the building so you can replace all the guards and alarms? Not OK.

TRAVEL EXPENSES

As all orders must be completed in 30 minutes or less, significant travel is unlikely to occur. In the event a ninja must board a plane, bus, taxi, train, or ferry, the ninja may write off the cost of the ticket or fare, provided it is at the lowest available rate. The ninja may NOT write off the cost of drinks, meals, or first-class upgrades.[7] In all cases, ninja are on their own for exiting such vehicles once they are in motion. Parachutes, lifejackets, etc. are advisable.

---

6 Of course, ninja are welcome to spend their OWN money to purchase items needed during a delivery.
7 Except, of course, in cases where the "obnoxious crying baby" exemption comes into play.

HONORABLE EMPLOYEE HANDBOOK

DISPATCH PROTOCOL

Dispatchers are given the job of coordinating the activities of several hundred delivery ninja, two dozen ninja cooks, and a garage full of ninja crew, while fielding one hundred calls an hour from customers. It's not just a job. It's an insane job—just take a look at the dispatch log on the next page.

Still think you can handle it? Then read on.

RADIO SHORTHAND

Every second counts to a delivery ninja team that is evading certain death, so dispatchers must be certain to communicate clearly and quickly. Here is some common "Radio Ninja" shorthand you might find useful:

SHORTHAND	TRANSLATION
Code Blue	Burger and/or fries are getting cold
Code Green	"All clear"; no obstacles, security, or enemies spotted
Code Black	Oops! There were obstacles, security, or enemies after all
Code Red	Ninja hurt, or too much ketchup (depends on context)
A.F.K.	Delivery Ninja missing (i.e., Away From Katana)
O.M.G. S.T.F.U.	Oscillating Micro-Grill w/ Supplemental Thermo-Fry Unit
R.I.P.	Order took longer than 30 minutes to deliver

FLEET COORDINATION

Dispatchers must be certain to match the delivery with the ninja delivery team best suited to handle the mission. For small orders delivered within a radius of a few miles, a single ninja on a motorcycle is usually adequate, whereas a full-blown infiltration into a locked, heavily secured building may call for a four-ninja team in a Ninja Burger shapeshifter delivery van.

Reserve boats and aircraft for emergencies. Sure, Toshiro wants to take a helicopter, but do the Lintons really want us landing on their roof?

SPECIAL DELIVERIES

Most deliveries will be to a home or business within a few miles, involving a few guard dogs, security systems, police and SWAT activity, and the like. At times Dispatch may discover yet more dangers, such as volcanoes, crocodiles, radiation leaks, samurai, poison gas, pirates, enemy ninja, etc. In these situations, use D.T.T.[8] protocol when speaking to delivery ninja; otherwise they might want hazard pay.

8 "Don't Tell Them."

43

NINJA BURGER

NINJA BURGER DISPATCH

Log # 01123341R55
Dispatcher on Call: Lee Garvin

Most Honorable Dispatcher: Thank you for calling Ninja Burger Delivery, please hold. Thank you for calling Ninja Burger Delivery, please hold. Delivery team Tetsubo, that order for the Baldwin compound has 4 minutes left! Chop-chop or it's chop-chop! Thank you for calling Ninja Burger delivery, what would you like to order?

Caller #1: Uh, yeah, I need 6 large Ninja Burgers, two large fries, and a Samurai Shake.

MHD: Fool! Samurai Shakes are the vile product of our most hated competitor! Perhaps you would like a Ninjacino instead?

C1: Uh, yeah, OK, whatever. I'm at—

MHD: Do not bother! We already know where you are and your order is on its way. Your total for 6 Ninja-Burgers, two large fries, and a Ninjacino is $19.68. As always, if your food is not there in 30 minutes, your delivery ninja will commit seppuku. As an apology for confusing us with those dishonorable dogs at that other chain, your delivery ninja will collect your left pinky finger. I suggest you do not resist . . .

C1: (Whimpering noise) <disconnect>

MHD: Maintenance, Ninja-Sat 18's picture is looking a bit fuzzy; have someone go EVA and fix it, would you? Thank you for holding, what would you like to order?

Caller #2: Hello, I already ordered, but I wanted to file a complaint.

MHD: Oh! Please accept my most humble apologies, ma'am! Was the delivery ninja late? (Sound of ninja-to being partially drawn from scabbard.)

C2: Oh, goodness, no! It was right on time and piping hot.

MHD: Then may I humbly ask what the problem is, most honorable customer? (Sound of ninja-to being snapped back into scabbard)

C2: Well, it's just that when Jeremy, our doorman, asked him for some identification, your ninja gave him a spin-kick that put him through the wall of the apartment next door.

MHD: Yes, ma'am; here at Ninja Burger we let nothing delay us in getting your food into your hands. Had Jeremy succeeded in stopping our ninja, your food might be a full five degrees cooler. You would have steaming entrails and a lifeless ninja in your foyer instead of your neighbors having an unconscious servant lodged in their wall. So, in the final analysis, you must agree this is the better outcome?

C2: Well, when you put it that way . . .

MHD: Excellent! Please call again.

C2: But—<disconnect>

MHD: Jerusalem branch, be sure the Prime Minister's meal is kosher; we don't want to repeat last week's fiasco. Thank you for calling Ninja Burger Delivery, please hold. Thank you for holding, what would you like to order?

Caller #3: (Silence)

MHD: Hello? Is there anybody there?

C3: (Silence)

MHD: Inzo? Is that you? If it is, be silent; if it isn't, say nothing.

C3: (Silence)

MHD: Inzo, I knew it was you. Your commitment to total stealth brings a tear to my eye.

C3: (Silence)

MHD: Are you at the delivery location? Do you require assistance?

C3: (Silence)

MHD: I have a customer service emergency team chopper nearby. What sort of assistance do you need? Long pause for a diversion, short pause for combat assistance.

C3: (Long pause)

MHD: All right, then, one diversion is en route. <channel change>

MHD: CSE Team Yohei! Delivery ninja Inzo is in a difficult spot and requires a distraction. Alter your flight plan to grid seven-four. The security force on the premises needs something else to worry about for the next 23 seconds.

Team Yohei Leader: Hai, dispatcher! We are in position! I will remain on air for further instructions as necessary.

44

(Sound of helicopter engine, static)

MHD: Team Yohei! Team Yohei! Are you there? Come in! <channel change>

TYL: (Muffled) Go! Go! Go! (Sound of automatic weapons fire) Fox one! (Sound of missile being launched, explosion, and what sounds like a late-model mini-van falling to the ground from a height of about 15 feet) Our principal is moving! Wow! Look at him go! (Sound of return fire, ricochet off surface close to the microphone) We're taking fire! I'm hit but it's not bad! We definitely have their attention! (Automatic weapons fire continues) Look out! They have anti- (Sound of missile being launched from ground) <disconnect>

MHD: Bring up Ninja-Sat 4. Focus camera on grid seven-four. Okay, there's the chopper, burning. I count 1 . . . 2 . . . 3 . . . dead ninja on the ground, but did Inzo make it? Wait! Zoom in and enhance on the upper left quadrant. Yes! A confused looking customer holding a Ninja-Burger bag, and Inzo is nowhere in sight! Damn, he's good! <channel change>

MHD: Good work, people, this is what we got into the business for. Branch manager, Tokyo is on line 3; they have some suggestions for how to get ectoplasm out of ninja suits. Thank you for holding. What would you like to order?

Caller #4: Oh, God, you've got to help me!

MHD: And what would you like help with, sir?

C4: I'm calling from my cell phone. I've been kidnapped by aliens! Please, I just want to go home.

MHD: I am most dreadfully sorry, sir, but you have reached Ninja Burger Delivery. We are not in a position to perform rescue operations. Perhaps a piping hot Ninja Burger, fries, and a cola would soothe your nerves?

C4: What? Are you kidding? They're going to probe me again! They'll be back here any minute now, and I think they want more samples.

MHD: Yes, those rectal probes can be quite bothersome. So what would you like to order?

C4: Uhh, A double-bacon Ninja Burger with hot wasabi sauce and a large order of jalapeno poppers. Yeah, that's it.

MHD: That's the spirit; if a rectal probe is unpleasant for you, it might as well be unpleasant for them. Your order will be there in 30 minutes or the delivery ninja will commit seppuku.

C4: Uh, thanks. <disconnect>

MHD: Thank you for calling Ninja Burger Delivery, please hold. Thank you for calling Ninja Burger. Delivery, please hold. Thank you for calling Ninja Burger. Delivery, what would you like to order?

Caller #5: Yeah, it's "you know who" again. Me and the joint chiefs are pulling an all-nighter, so I'll need the usual, delivered to the war room.

MHD: Most certainly, sir! (over intercom) All available ninjas! We have a code W! Repeat. We have a code W!

C5: Domo oregano. <disconnect>

MHD: Thank you for holding. What would you like to order?

Caller #6: <silence>

MHD: Inzo! I'm so glad you're OK! I have a very difficult delivery for you; is your spacesuit in good repair?

C6: <silence>

MHD: Good, good.

END LOGFILE.

ADVANCED DELIVERY TACTICS

If you made it this far, you've learned how to hide. There's absolutely no other way you would have survived Invisibility 101.[9] You have also already learned in Stealth 101[10] how to move to avoid detection. And in Infiltration 101 which completes the triad of Basic Delivery Training, you learned how to disable security devices, enter locked buildings, and incapacitate guards.

You didn't know about that class? Too late! Time to put that knowledge (or lack thereof) to the test! Invisibility, stealth, and infiltration skills mean nothing when you've got 45 seconds to reach the 26th floor.

MODERN STEALTH TECHNIQUES

Modern buildings are chock full of little nooks and crannies to hide in. Our ancestors may have had to crawl around beneath bamboo outhouses, but we've got it good compared to them.

Need to move between floors in an unseen fashion? Look for the main wet wall (the one with pipes in it) and climb around at your leisure. Or how about those dropped ceiling panels that everyone has—there's like two feet of clearance up there. Just watch out for dust bunnies. In a pinch, you can even try the Dai-Hardu maneuver, and crawl around inside the air vents.[11]

REACHING NEW HEIGHTS

One of your biggest challenges will be delivering to high places, be they tall buildings, high mountains, or hot air balloons.

Carefully consider all your options before you begin your ascent. Elevator in service? Try the stairs. Is the lobby full of guards? Blow them away, climb up the elevator shaft, blow up the lobby, fight your way to the roof, steal a helicopter, and fly back down to the floor your customer is on. Or, you could just start from the top to begin with. Going down is easier than going up.[12]

9 Not only is attendance not mandatory, but it's discouraged. Master Li says: "If I see you in class, you're dead."
10 Always the worst-attended class in basic training. Students automatically pass the class if they know it exists.
11 When delivering to a building full of terrorists, avoid rooms with large glass windows. Terrorists like to shoot these out, and you're not wearing any shoes.
12 Unless you're delivering to a submarine. Ninja tend to float.

UNCOMMON SENSE

Your ninja skills may help you complete your mission, but sometimes you'll need to rely on something that no one can teach you[13]—common sense. Fire is hot. Water is wet. Ninja cannot walk through walls or fly.[14]

But some things aren't obvious. For example, elevators: with the amount of time it takes to change floors, it's usually faster to take the stairs. Elevators aren't time-savers for late people. They're energy-savers for lazy people.

And don't get us started on sewers. From what you see on TV, they're big enough to drive a truck down, and inhabited by turtles. The truth is usually they're not even big enough for a child. Not to mention, it's not hygenic to take food down there.

Other "uncommon" commonsense things you should keep in mind:

- It's impossible to sneeze with your eyes open. Security guards plus sneezing powder = your chance to sneak by.
- If a goldfish sees you, don't panic. Their memory lasts 30 seconds. However, dolphins sleep with one eye open. Don't trust dolphins.
- Nobody will question your presence if you have a badge, a clipboard, or a pair of brown shorts, provided you remove your mask first.
- Since a cat always lands with its feet down, a cat dropped on a guard will land claws-first on the guard's head.
- Since most accidents occur in a person's own home, fight enemies on their home turf where odds are in your favor.

BREAKING THE RULES

At times, you will need to forget what you've been taught and do the exact opposite.

For example, ninja should try to avoid capture, but if the delivery is to a prisoner, getting captured might be a good idea.

Ninja should also avoid being seen, but a team member might choose to be seen in order to conceal another ninja's presence, as on an airplane, bus, subway or other public transportation (see image to right).

In short, any rule may be broken if it helps the delivery[15].

13 Not that we haven't tried. Common Sense 101 appeared on our class schedule for five years. Unfortunately, every ninja who attended the class completely lacked any (common sense, that is), and we had a 100 percent casualty rate.
14 See Footnote 1.
15 Except the one about accepting tips. NO TIPS.

DRIVER PROTOCOL

If ninja deliverators are the public face of Ninja Burger, then our ninja drivers are the legs and feet. Without them, most delivery ninja would have no chance of arriving at their destinations within 30 minutes, and Ninja Burger would have a much higher turnover rate than it already does.

Many ninja compete each year for the chance to be ninja drivers. The benefits of the job are obvious. As long as you get to the delivery location within 30 minutes, any failed delivery is not your fault, and so the seppuku rule does not apply. Also, while your deliverators are out being chased by dogs, climbing up the sides of buildings, and otherwise facing near death, you get to chill in the van and listen to the radio.

However, drivers do have a special set of rules they must abide by.

~~BREAKING~~ BENDING THE LAW

Ninja Burger does not condone, authorize, or in any way encourage drivers to break the law while making a delivery. Exceeding the speed limit, changing lanes illegally, weaving erratically, etc., are all WRONG and SHOULD NOT BE DONE under any circumstances.

However, note that as with delivery ninja, Ninja Burger also disavows all knowledge and responsibility for ninja teams who are out on deliveries. So technically, since you don't exist, we can't tell you what to do. Hint, hint.

UNACCEPTABLE BEHAVIOR

Ninja Burger does not condone behavior which unnecessarily puts any team member or customer in danger. Drivers are tested at the beginning of each shift to ensure that they are not under the influence of illegal substances. However, being under the influence of sugar and caffeine from Ninja Cola is fine.

Ninja drivers should also avoid endangering, or being seen by, other drivers. Endangering the lives of your teammates is one thing—they're not expected to live very long anyway—but you should never put a member of the public at risk. Remember, everyone on the road is a potential customer, and a happy customer is one who's not suing us (assuming they can find us, of course).

LAST RESORTS

If delivery ninja are incapacitated or terminated, it is the responsibility of the driver to complete a delivery, whether or not there is time left. It is also his responsibility to make a "best effort" to extract lost teammates before returning to base. No leaving rookies behind; it's funny but it kills the training budget.

DRIVER TRAINING

All ninja drivers must complete 100 hours of training as a copilot/navigator prior to being allowed to serve as lead driver on any delivery mission. This includes solo missions requiring a vehicle—new delivery ninja who are sent on single-person missions will need to use other means of transportation, such as taking a bus, calling a taxi, or just running with super ninja speed.

All potential drivers must have a valid driver's license, without any traffic infractions, and proof of insurance. Obviously we already know about your driving record, so you don't have to show these things to us. Should you lack a license or insurance, but still want to participate, you are welcome to join our Crash Test division. They're always in need of fresh blood, so to speak.

When selecting ninja drivers, preference will be given to the following:

- Former NASCAR , Formula-1, or other race car drivers
- Former police officers, EMTs, or firefighters
- Former Hollywood movie stunt drivers
- Former New York City cab drivers

NINJA H.U.D.

All ninja drivers and navigators will be trained in the use of our specialized Heads-Up Display technology.[16] Built into the windshield of all vehicles, as well as special goggles, sunglasses, and helmets, the display gives driver and navigator a unique view of the road ahead, displaying speed, direction, and time remaining for the delivery, as well as information about other vehicles.

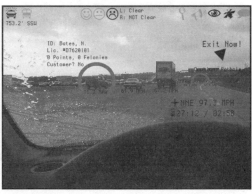

This information is updated in real time through uplinks to both Dispatch and our satellite network, allowing our drivers to react instantaneously to avoid traffic snarls, police speed traps, chickens crossing the road, etc.

VEHICLE MAINTENANCE

While ninja crew are primarily responsible for the refueling and maintaining of our fleet of vehicles, it is the responsibility of the vehicle's primary driver to check his van, car, or other transport before each shift to ensure it is in proper working order. Since ninja crew are often in line for jobs as ninja drivers (which are in short supply), drivers should take extra care to check for things such as cut brake lines, bombs under the dashboard, etc.

---

16 Ninja who are joining us from the military may be familiar with this, since we have licensed it to the Air Force.

DEALING WITH THE LAW

You may have noticed that despite all the reality shows on television, there has yet to be a *World's Most Dangerous Ninja Chases*. This is in part because our drivers are so skilled at evading authorities, and, in part, because the owners of all the major TV networks are our customers.

However, despite your best efforts, there may come a time when you, as a ninja driver, are forced to deal with the authorities. For those situations, we offer the following guidelines.

RESPONSIBILITY

Remember how earlier we said you had to have a license and insurance? Remember how we said we'd not even acknowledge you exist? Well, we meant it. If you are unlucky enough to get into an accident, or be pulled over by the cops, you alone will be responsible for getting yourself out of the mess. You, Señor Jebediah Gonzalez, who lives at 123 Fake Street in Whatchamacallit, North Dakota.

Get the picture?

PARKING TICKETS

The best way to avoid getting a parking citation is, of course, not to park.[17] Circle the block if possible, letting your deliverators roll or jump out the back of your moving delivery van.[18] If you must park, remember to disguise your vehicle, and park in a place where you can make a quick getaway. A garbage truck driven by a ninja on the fifth floor of a parking ramp is going to stand out more than a little bit in most neighborhoods.

SPEEDING TICKETS

You will probably be speeding most of the time you're in your vehicle. In major metropolitan areas, this will be less noticeable, since everyone else will be speeding as well, but in the event a police officer pulls you over, try the following excuses to explain your situation:

- Late for a costume party.
- On way to a mime's convention, so cannot speak (difficult to pull off).
- A new kind of super hero, and Dr. Disgusto is ravaging downtown!
- Looking for a better job? See, my employer is hiring people like you.
- Friend of Michael Jackson.

17 Easy enough in San Francisco or New York City, since in those cities parking isn't even an option.
18 Not recommended at high speeds or on narrow bridges.

PERSONAL USE OF VEHICLES

When vehicles from our fleet are not in active use in our regular delivery rotation, they may be available for personal use by Ninja Burger employees. Such vehicles may be checked out with Dispatch and, upon being cleared by Ninja Crew and your supervisor, may be used freely with the following limits.

AUTHORIZED USES

Official Ninja Burger vehicles may be used for the following purposes:

- Transportation between work and home, or work and a restaurant.
- Emergency transportation to a doctor, hospital, or to save a family member who has been abducted and held for ransom by pirates.
- Trips to a gas station or garage to pick up/drop off an employee's car.
- Team-building activities, such as miniature golf or karaoke.
- Shopping trips for groceries or gifts, provided that the employees also pick up some milk for their supervisor, and a candy bar for Dispatch.

UNAUTHORIZED USES

Official Ninja Burger vehicles may NOT be used for the following purposes:

- Visiting a competing fast-food chain (unless it's to wage war).
- Any activity described as too fast and/or too furious.
- Cruising for chicks/dudes. ("Hey baby, I'm a ninja. Want a ride?")
- Anything involving tankers full of gas and angry Australian mutants.
- "Just wanted to see how fast it would go."

PIMPING YOUR RIDE

Ninja Burger encourages drivers to customize and personalize their primary vehicles with their own funds and on their own time, to help foster a sense of team unity and to keep budget costs down. Employees may hang fuzzy dice, install upgraded sound systems, put in DVD players and television screens, and otherwise trick out their interiors. Adding high-performance tires, amped-up engines, and bulletproof glass are also encouraged.

However, the following are prohibited on Ninja Burger vehicles:

- Paint. Ninja Burger vehicles are all painted with a special paint which can change color to match surroundings and evade pursuit.
- Unnecessary spoilers or dual exhaust. We don't need to pretend our vehicles are faster than they are. They really are faster than they are.
- Ninja-on-board signs.
- Type-R stickers on non Type-R vehicles. There are no Type-R vans.
- Lasers or machine guns.
- Anything with a turret, basically.

"EIGHT WEEKS AGO, I WELCOMED **420** RECRUITS, AND I WEPT OPENLY, LIKE A SMALL CHILD. I THOUGHT NONE OF YOU WOULD SURVIVE. BUT I AM PLEASED TO SEE THAT I WAS WRONG. AND SO NOW, AS I CALL YOUR NAME, PLEASE COME UP TO ACCEPT YOUR DIPLOMA."

—NINJA RECRUIT PÉPÉ HABAÑERO

"**OK**, WELL, THAT WRAPS IT UP FOR THIS YEAR."

—NINJA DEAN ANDER-SAN

Honorable Employee Handbook

5: Employee Guidelines

You survived basic training, you made it through cooking class without being blinded by hot grease, and delivery class didn't result in your self-disembowelment. Congratulations—you're officially a full-blown Ninja Burger employee. But to quote Sensei Holo-san: "Great, kid, great . . . don't get cocky."

Not only will you have to remember everything you were taught to this point and put it into practice on a daily basis, but you have a whole new set of rules and regulations to learn. This section explains the basics.

Questions about how to interpret the policies that follow should be directed to your manager or the highest-ranking ninja on duty within your franchise, to include your delivery team lead. If no superior is available, act as your ninja skills suggest. If you're wrong, of course, you'll have to commit seppuku, but try not to stress over it. We encourage a stress-free workplace.

Terms of Employment

We practice "at-will employment," which means that your employment is at our will. Ninja Burger may terminate you at any time, and you are free to terminate yourself. You just can't ever quit. Grounds for termination include:

- Failure to deliver an order in 30 minutes or less
- Being dishonorable to your ancestors or employer
- Stealing extra wasabi packets
- Being caught on film (e.g., appearing on *World's Funniest Videos*)
- Doing business with the enemy (you do NOT deserve a break today)

For a complete list of all situations, which are grounds for termination, please see Guide #NB404, "Seppuku & You: 50 Ways to Leave Your Life."[1] For more about termination, see the last page of this guide.

Employee Equipment Package

As a trainee, you got a standard-issue ninja uniform. As a full employee, you also receive the following:

- Ninja Burger ID card
- Ninja Burger GPS receiver/locator
- A free T-shirt
- Security pass, level C (Cook), D1 (Delivery), or D2 (Dispatch)
- A pair of spatulas (Cook), swords (Delivery), or fuzzy dice (Driving)
- Two movie passes, and a coupon for a free order of fries (small)

Additional gear (smokebombs, shuriken, soy sauce, etc.) will be made available on an as-needed basis, depending on your mission and work schedule.

1. Method #1: Slip a sword in your back, Jack; Method #4: Jump in front of a bus, Gus; etc.

NINJA BURGER

NINJA ARCHIVE DIVISION

The Ninja Archive Division (N.A.D.) maintains the central Ninja Burger database that tracks all company information, from customer purchase records, to accounting logs, to employee personnel information. Through ties to the Internet, Internet 2, Internet 3, the CIA, FBI, MI-5, Billboard, Warehouse 23, Echelon, Val-Mart, and several other organizations, Ninja Burger is able to accurately track all employees and customers (past, present, and future).

So we not only know where you live, but what you ate for dinner.[2]

ARCHIVE SECURITY

Obviously, anyone with access to our database would be able to wield tremendous influence, which is why Ninja Burger safeguards this information with several layers of security. For example, the data is triple-encrypted with 50-digit randomized passwords, which are changed every 23 hours.

Because computers are fallible, human beings are also part of the equation. The N.A.D. is headed by a Board of Governing Officers who operate autonomously and anonymously. We don't know who they are; only they know.[3] Every year, they gather to choose amongst themselves who will serve as Governing Officers of N.A.D. Security; of the twenty members chosen to serve, only two survive the selection process. Each of these individuals memorizes half of a six-hundred word passphrase, combining words from twelve different languages. Only with the two G.O.N.A.D.S. working together in unison can the central Ninja Archives be accessed.[4]

RIGHT TO PRIVACY

Ninja Burger never shares anything with anyone outside Ninja Burger, so don't worry about that, first of all. You don't exist, remember?

That said, there may be times when information about Ninja Burger Employees (perhaps the deceased "you," or perhaps one of your new identities) might be accessed by another individual or organization. You will always be notified about such access attempts, unless of course it's because you did something bad, in which case you probably already know they're after you.

Ninja Burger can help ensure your right to total privacy by occasionally making problems "go away." We automatically do this for you when you are hired by erasing your old life. From time to time, we may also assist in doing this with regards to any new identity you've adopted. However, Ninja Burger will not intervene in the following matters:

• Matters of national security, treason or terrorism
• Late library books or DVD rentals

---

2 We're also tied into the secret Central Repository Archive of Plumbers (C.R.A.P.).
3 Unless, of course, they are us, in which case we do know. Either way, we're not telling. And neither are they.
4 However, because cooks, dispatchers, and delivery ninja need to access this data rapidly throughout the day, a backup security system has been put in place in every Ninja Burger computer terminal, vehicle, cell phone, PDA, and fax machine. The password is "Ninja-123." Don't tell anyone.

Personnel Records

What does Ninja Burger know about you? It's pretty safe to assume the answer is "everything." But in case you're curious, paranoid or wondering what you can get away with, here's a brief list of some of the data we keep:

- Hiring and recruitment
- Job duties and classification
- Rate of pay and benefits
- Advanced training and education
- Honors and awards (if any)
- Performance reviews and attendance records
- List of dishonorable actions (kept with a small baggie of your fingers)

Changes in Your Personnel File

All records are expected to be maintained in an accurate, timely, and complete fashion. Any omissions or errors are assumed to be the responsibility of the employee, so you are expected to review your files every few weeks to make sure things are in order and make additions, deletions, or corrections.

Employees may visit the N.A.D. any time from Monday through Tuesday between 6:30 A.M. and 6:45 A.M.

Contact Information

Being ninja, you are expected to regularly adopt new identities. Try to keep your records up-to-date by providing your current alias, address, telephone number, and other information. This is in part so we can help cover for you if need be and also so we can come looking for you if you betray us.

Marital Status

Although it doesn't happen too often, sometimes ninja fall in love with the man/woman who tried to kill them, and decide to get married. Should you decide to take the leap, please notify us as soon as possible, so we can update your records and run a background check on your new spouse.

Dependents

Should marriage lead to, well, you know what, then let us know so we can adjust your records and take efforts to protect your family should an enemy swear a blood oath on your kin. You'd be surprised how often that happens. Well, maybe not.

WORK SCHEDULE

All employees, regardless of their position in the company, will be assigned to work at one particular Ninja Burger franchise. You will be expected to report to work within five minutes of your scheduled shift on every day that you are scheduled to work. No "working from home."[5]

When you are on the job (whether that's in your franchise, in a vehicle, or on a delivery in a customer location), you are expected to be doing nothing other than your assigned duties. If you have no assigned duties (i.e., you're waiting for a delivery to come in), you are expected to be training, studying, or cleaning something.

Don't make us find something for you to clean. Trust us. We can find something, and you won't like it.

STANDARD SHIFT

Ninja Burger is open 24 hours a day, 7 days a week, 365 days a year. To cover the needs of our customers who call in at all hours of the day and night, we have a series of overlapping 8-, 10- and 12-hour shifts which rotate new ninja in and out every two hours throughout the day.

Normally, ninja work five 8-hour shifts or four 10-hour shifts in any given week, plus overtime. This does not include time you are expected to be training, studying or cleaning things, which should occupy at least another 40 to 50 hours a week. Budget for this extra time. A ninja who is not constantly honing skills is a ninja who will soon be honing his wakizashi for seppuku.

HOLIDAYS

Ninja Burger never closes, but we know that employees might wish to take holidays off, even if their entire family was murdered by pirates and/or samurai. As needed, we will shuffle your schedule around. Just don't take off for Christmas, Hanukkah, and Kwanzaa all at once.[6] See the section on "Paid Time Off" for more.

CLOCK CHANGES

Every year daylight saving time confuses everyone in the spring and the fall. To avoid further confusion, Ninja Burger has instituted the following policy: On days when the clocks shift, everyone has to work two extra hours.

5 We know you're not working. What, you think we're stupid?
6 No one, especially ninja, should be that jolly.

JURY DUTY

While voting, military duties, being sued, etc., aren't an issue (you're dead), not even a ninja can get out of jury duty, and we will not count it as a negative mark in your file should you need time off for this.

Ninja Burger encourages our ninja to serve on a jury when called, in part because it's a civic duty, yadda-yadda, but also for two very good reasons. First, it never hurts to do the court system a favor now and then. And since we do occasionally work within shady areas of the law, our ninja should be well aware of the legal system, so they can avoid being caught within it.

Secondly, juries get hungry, and there's no better customer for us than a sequestered jury foreman. Note that Ninja Burger does not reimburse our employees for time served on a jury, unless you manage to convince the jury to order food. So you should try your hardest.

EMPLOYEE MEALS AND BREAKS

We never know when the president is going to call from the middle of the jungle under heavy rocket bombardment with an urgent delivery that has a 10-minute window, so we cannot give employees scheduled breaks.

However, your work schedule is such that you should be able to find plenty of downtime to grab a bite to eat, listen to some music, meditate, etc., whether it's in the employee break room while waiting for an order to come in, or in the back of the van on the way to the delivery. You may take up to 30 minutes worth of "break time" for an 8-hour shift, and an additional 15 minutes for each 2 hours worked thereafter.

Employees may dine for free up to three times per day at the employee cafeteria, or by placing an order in the normal fashion. Orders that exceed this will be deducted from your paycheck, or your neck, as appropriate.

OVERTIME

In the event of a crunch, your manager will be instructed by her supervisor to dole out overtime. All employees are expected to work any assigned overtime, not to exceed twice their original scheduled shift. So if you really don't want to work overtime be sure to practice your stealth skills.

Ninja Burger employees who are classified as "exempt" from overtime pay do not receive extra pay for overtime. This includes all employees in HR, administrative or executive positions, which means about seventeen people total in the whole company, really. The majority of Ninja Burger employees are classified as "non-exempt," which means they do earn additional pay for overtime. Cooks, Deliverators, drivers, and dispatchers are all paid at their base pay rate for this additional time, NOT time-and-a-half or double-time. Want more money for the same work? Then impress us and earn a raise.

SALARY AND BENEFITS

Ninja Burger's policy is to entice skilled employees to join us through exciting work, a good benefits package, and a generous salary. Flexible scheduling and the opportunity for unlimited overtime, free of any federal regulations, means that our employees can determine for themselves how much they want to work and how much they want to earn. We believe our benefits and salary are the best in the industry. And who else lets you work while wearing a sword?

SALARY AND GROSS PAY

All new ninja employees start out at our standard salary rate, which is twice the minimum wage applicable to that particular franchise, based on the highest rate as determined by federal, state, county, and city standards.

Over time, salary adjustments will be made based strictly on the skill and dedication of the individual employee; there are no automatic raises over time, save for minor increases to the base rate to match any fluctuation in the minimum wage. Often such adjustments will be made in concordance with an official change in title or position.

Employees are paid from the moment security cameras pick them up upon arrival at work (remember to "turn off" the stealth or you won't get paid) until the moment of their scheduled departure or unconsciousness,[7] whichever comes first. Gross pay is thus determined by multiplying the employee's base salary by the number of hours and minutes worked.

Exempt ninja are paid at a base rate that is not tied to the minimum wage, but you won't ever become one of those, so don't worry about it.

PAYROLL ADJUSTMENTS

After a ninja's gross pay has been computed, adjustments are made in the form of bonuses (rare) or deductions (not rare). Bonuses may be awarded for achieving company goals, performing a hazardous delivery (Hazard Pay), referring an employee,[8] or through recommendation by a customer.

Deductions[9] to an employee's gross pay may include:

- Parking permit fees (if applicable)
- Dorm fees (if employee lives in company-sponsored housing)
- Meal fees (if more than three free meals per day are eaten)
- Employer-sponsored health coverage fees (discussed later)
- Employee Activities Fee (discussed later)
- Other fees (e.g., damages to vehicles, lost equipment, etc.)

---

7 Employees who fall unconscious due to work-related illness, injury, or fatigue are not paid for the duration of their unconsciousness, though they are still eligible to receive benefits such as the use of our infirmary.
8 Bonuses of 5 percent of the base starting salary are given if someone you refer survives 30 days as an employee.
9 Note that since technically you don't exist, taxes are never withheld from your paycheck.

HONORABLE EMPLOYEE HANDBOOK

PAYDAY

All employees are paid 24 times per year, which breaks down to twice per month: on the 14th and the 28th.[10] Payment is issued on these days regardless of day of the week, holidays, or any other circumstances. Paychecks received on the 14th will include payment for work done on the 29th, 30th, and 31st of the previous month if applicable.

DIRECT DEPOSIT

Ninja Burger prefers to deposit payment via an electronic transfer to one or more bank accounts of your choice, as this means less paper that has to be shredded by the Accounting department after the fact. As we already know, if you have a bank account, we will automatically make a deposit to your most active account on your first payday. Should you wish to split your deposit, need assistance in setting up a Swiss bank account, or desire to make any other change, please speak with your manager.

Employees who wish to receive an actual paper paycheck can pick one up at the Accounting office after 9 A.M. on each payday. Employees will be charged a nominal fee[11] for this service.

PARKING PERMITS

Ninja employees who have their own vehicles are entitled to park on Ninja Burger property in reserved spots, provided they have elected to pay for a parking permit out of their paychecks. Permits are good for the period of time covered by the paycheck used to pay for them, and are automatically renewed until the employee turns in the permit. They are nontransferable.

Employees are free to park on surrounding streets and parking ramps if they do not wish to pay for parking, but they may not park in any spots reserved for customer use (despite the fact that most customers cannot find our well-concealed dine-in locations, because you never know).

10 It used to be the 15th and the 30th, but people complained they only got paid once in February.
11 50 percent of your gross pay, before deductions. You'll probably want to just go with electronic.

HEALTH SERVICES

Ninja Burger provides a unique service to our customers. This service may include situations that could prove hazardous to your health or the health of others. These include: capture by enemy; attack by Samurai; poison by rogue ninja; temptation by nubile female ninja; falling off walls; falling into spiked pits; being decapitated; grease burns; and salmonella poisoning.

Ninja Burger realizes that a healthy employee is a functionally capable employee. We do our best to respond to health needs and ensure a safe workplace whenever possible; thus, we have established the Department of Employee and Trainee Health Services. They are ultimately responsible for implementing safety and health policies at our many franchises, with some five-hundred country- and region-level safety officers assisting in the posting, enforcement, and testing[12] of those policies and procedures in each and every Ninja Burger franchise.

On the following pages are some of our key policies in this area.

MEDICAL FACILITIES

While Ninja Burger does not offer health insurance, all employees are eligible for 100 precent free service at any Ninja Burger medical facility. Each franchise maintains a clinic staffed by a trained RN,[13] and each regional center has more advanced medical facilities, ranging from allergy, physical therapy, and psychiatric services, to fully-staffed surgical departments for more dire needs.

All facilities are available to all ninja at all times, including off-work hours, though you should be aware that we follow a strict triage protocol. Those with minor injuries (missing limbs, third-degree burns, etc.) may have to wait while ninja with more life-threatening conditions are treated first.

12 As testing the efficacy of safety and health procedures requires violation of those procedures in the first place, Ninja Burger's D.E.A.T.H.S. is currently in need of 500 additional staff. Ask your Department Head for more info.
13 "Random Ninja."

DENTAL/VISION SERVICES

Ninja must always maintain anonymity. As being fitted for glasses or having teeth fixed requires mask removal, Ninja Burger can provide a list of dentists and optometrists who are either visually impaired, or willing to perform their services wearing a blindfold.

Employees must pay out-of-pocket for these services, but in the event of any unforeseen complications, our in-franchise health facilities will happily assist in dulling pain, staunching any bleeding, or providing you with a seeing-eye dog,[14] as necessary.

BLOOD BANK

Ninja Burger maintains a blood and organ bank for emergency use when situations call for it.[15] All employees are asked to donate blood once a month to keep stocks high, in addition to the normal requirement that you donate all blood and organs[16] to the bank in the event of death while on the job.

COUNSELING SERVICES

Being a ninja is hard. We know. Really, we do. We're ninja. So we know what it's like to run around on a 30-minute-or-die schedule, while everyone from security guards to police to angry dogs (and occasionally, fellow employees) is trying to kill you. That's why Ninja Burger now provides employees with reliable, friendly, confidential counseling and mental health services.

Employees who are having problems, including those related to work stress, substance abuse, legal concerns, emotional distress, death threats, or existential dilemmas, are invited to visit with one of our counselors, who can offer an individual or group therapy session to help you with your problem. Employees who require more than one session will get special assistance in dealing with their problem, explained on page 76.

SMOKE-FREE ENVIRONMENT

Ninja Burger does not permit smoking[17] inside any of our vehicles or facilities. Ninja may smoke during break time in designated outdoor areas, out of sight of customers, but in general smoking is discouraged, because it makes stealth difficult (e.g., clothes smell funny, cloud of smoke hovers overhead, camouflage catches fire, etc.). Should they wish to quit, Ninja Burger invites employees to attend a quarterly smoking cessation seminar.[18]

---

14 Not that this should ever be necessary, seeing as you are a ninja, after all.
15 Pretty often, as you may have figured out.
16 At least, what's left. There's "dead," and then there's "organs cannot be found."
17 This does not include occupational smoke from grilling burgers, throwing smoke bombs, or catching on fire.
18 The seminar consists of a ninja shouting, "You will stop smoking, or I will kill you!." If you don't, he does.

NINJA BURGER

FIRST-AID CHART

As health facilities may not always be close at hand (especially when you're delivering burgers atop Mount Everest), ninja employees should learn to identify injuries, determine their degree of severity, and respond appropriately.

Use the following chart to determine what action to take depending on the circumstances involved:

INJURY	APPROPRIATE ACTION
Paper cut	Quit whining, get back to work.
Knife cut	Wash in sink, dry well, disinfect the knife, and try not to bleed on anything while you do it.
Sword cut	Bind wound tightly, enter meditative trance to slow heart and blood flow, commune with dead ancestors.
Seppuku cut	Die quickly and your ancestors will be honored.
Minor burn	Apply burn pad, cover with gauze, get back to work.
Major burn	As above, but seek medical attention after shift ends.
Really major burn	As above, but seek medical attention after delivery is finished or order is done cooking.
Broken finger	You have nine fingers left; we don't see the problem here.
Broken hand/arm	Splint and bind to side, avoid using, seek medical attention when shift ends.
Broken leg/foot	Use crane-stance technique, as taught in the film *The Karate Kid*; you have seen it, right?
Two broken arms/legs	Now you're just being difficult, aren't you?
Headache, tension	Take two aspirin and call us in the morning.
Headache, sinus	Take two aspirin and call us in the morning.
Headache, migraine	Take two aspirin and call us in the morning.
Stomach pain, mild	Stop taking so much aspirin.
Stomach pain, severe	Alien infestation; drink milk, avoid populated areas.

SICKNESS/DISEASE IDENTIFICATION CHART

Since ninja delivery personnel are required to deliver all over the world, to customers who may at times be indisposed by illness, it is possible that they will encounter or be exposed to various diseases. Ninja should learn to identify these illnesses, so they may properly respond to them.

SYMPTOMS	APPROPRIATE ACTION
Sore throat, coughing, chills, headache, fever, malaise	Cold. Eat some chicken soup and wait it out.
Sore throat, coughing, chills, headache, fever, malaise	Flu. Drink some fluids and wait it out.
Sore throat, coughing, chills, headache, fever, malaise	Pneumonia. 99 percent chance of survival. Treat with IV fluids and antiviral medication.
Sore throat, coughing, chills, headache, fever, malaise	Bubonic plague. 40 percent chance of survival. Treat with antibiotics, isolate from other ninja.
Sore throat, coughing, chills, headache, fever, malaise	Ebola. 10 percent chance of survival, no treatment available. Pray to your ancestors.

HONORABLE EMPLOYEE HANDBOOK

WORKERS' COMPENSATION

Although it is unlikely (and discouraged), ninja employees may from time to time find themselves unable to work due to work-related injury or illness. In such cases, Ninja Burger will provide adequate workers' compensation to the ninja during his or her recovery.

Ninja Burger medical benefits, which cover employees at all times, have already been discussed and are not considered part of the compensation package itself. Items considered part of compensation include: 75 percent wage loss during short-term disability, up to 3 months; 25 percent wage loss during long-term disability, up to 6 months; and death benefits with a burial allowance in the event of permanent disability[19] or death.

"Disability" implies that a ninja employee is so badly injured or ill that they are unable to perform any job duties; it does not refer to what the public refers to as "disabilities," which Ninja Burger does not acknowledge (as explained earlier).

USING PTO FIRST

Employees are required to use any Paid Time Off (PTO) accrued before receiving compensation benefits. For example, a ninja who is taking two weeks of disability, but has one week of PTO accrued, must use their one week of PTO, after which they will be compensated for one week of disability.

Employees continue to accrue PTO during periods of disability, though they will only receive credit for the accrued time upon returning to work. Ninja who do not want to use their PTO for periods of disability should try really hard not to become disabled. For more on PTO, see the next page.

RETURNING TO WORK

Ninja Burger requires that all ninja employees who are on disability report in to work at least once per week so Ninja Burger doctors can assess their condition. Employees may be required to attend counseling or physical therapy sessions to assist in their recovery.

Employees who are deemed capable of returning to work will be required to report for their shift the day after being cleared. In general, employees are considered able if they meet the following criteria:

- Can hold a spatula or delivery bag in at least one hand
- Are conscious[20]

PERMANENT DISABILITY

Employees who are permanently disabled and unable to ever return to work will receive special assistance in dealing with their disability, explained on page 76 of this handbook.

---

19 You should really try and get better. Really.
20 Optional, depending on the circumstances and the ninja's job duties (as with ninja mental health counselors).

PAID TIME OFF (PTO)

Ninja Burger appreciates that employees occasionally need time off to deal with personal matters, whether that means polishing your sword or taking a vacation to your ancestors' burial ground. All "sick time," "personal days," and "vacation time" are rolled into a single category called Paid Time Off.

EARNED HOURS

Employees earn PTO based on the amount of paid hours they work for the company. All employees earn one hour of PTO per 16 hours worked, or roughly 10 hours per month given a standard work schedule.[21] The rate of accrual is the same for overtime hours. Employees who survive to serve the company for at least 5 years earn an additional 8 hours of PTO per year of service, starting with their fifth year. For example, a ninja who has worked for five years earns an additional 40 hours on top of his normal accrual, and a ninja who has worked 10 years earns an additional 80 hours.[22]

Accrued PTO caps at 80 hours (10 days); additional hours will not be accrued until some PTO is spent. Thus, employees are encouraged to take time off regularly to avoid losing PTO. You are not expected to survive long, so enjoy your vacation while you can. You can't visit Lake Tahoe in a coffin.[23]

VACATION LEAVE

When possible, ninja should provide at least two weeks (14 days) notice of their intent to take more than three days off in a row, and at least four weeks (28 days) notice of an intent to take more than six days off in a row.

Failure to provide adequate notice of such foreseeable events may result in postponement of the leave, disciplinary action, or termination. Note that employees who have honed their prophetic skills are required to give notice of every vacation they ever intend to take since it's all foreseeable.

SICKNESS OR BEREAVEMENT LEAVE

Ninja should give adequate notice of their intent to take time off for medical reasons, whether for medical appointments, "under-the-weather days," or "mental health days." However, we understand that at times, unexpected sickness does occur, and we follow a policy of encouraging sick ninja to rest and recuperate so as to avoid making other employees or customers sick.

However, we know if you are faking. And if you are faking sick, believe us, you won't be faking for long. Employees who take more than 2 days in a row as sick days will be required to provide proof of illness, in the form of a signed excuse from a Ninja Burger physician. Employees who require time off for bereavement (the death of a loved one) will be required to provide proof of bereavement in the form of a body (or an urn, as appropriate).

---

21 You will not have a standard work schedule. More likely, you will have two work schedules rolled into one.
22 As well as the admiration of his colleagues, since few ninja survive for longer than 10 months, much less years.
23 Well, you can, but the view isn't that great.

TIME OFF WITHOUT PAY (TOWP)

When absolutely necessary, employees may opt to take Time Off Without Pay if they have exhausted their PTO hours. In all such cases, TOWP requests should be made at least twenty-four hours prior to taking time off, and at the very latest no later than one hour after your shift was scheduled to begin.

LEAVE OF ABSENCE WITHOUT PAY

When necessary, and given adequate notice, employees may request a Leave of Absence Without Pay to take time off for: pregnancy, childbirth, family reasons, outside education/training that will improve job effectiveness, personal revenge/matters of honor, or "ninja stuff." As Ninja Burger always has openings for employees, returning to work after a leave is never an issue.

AWOL

Employees who fail to report to work as scheduled, and who fail to call in to request TOWP, will be considered AWOL (Absent WithOut Leave). Penalties for being AWOL for a day or two range from docked pay, to lost PTO, to termination (in extreme circumstances). Employees who are absent for extended periods of time without permission must provide a satisfactory explanation upon their return. As you are a ninja, it better be a good excuse.[24]

Unacceptable reasons for being AWOL include:

- Public emergencies (fire, explosion, flood, earthquake, nuclear war)
- Bad weather (snowstorm, tornado, hurricane, etc.)
- Trapped in a well
- Stuck in traffic
- Hung over a tank of sharks with laser beams attached to their heads

See the following diagram for a better illustration.

| **UNACCEPTABLE** | **UNACCEPTABLE** | **UNACCEPTABLE** | **ACCEPTABLE** |

---

24 i.e., You must provide a detailed account of the events leading up to your death.

FAMILY MATTERS

We know the importance of family. Our founders come from a long line of ninja, and we encourage our employees to continue to pass the way of the ninja down to new generations. Obviously, this requires that there be new ninja to pass things down to, and that's where family comes in.[25]

NINJA DAY CARE

Ninja who already have families of their own should never feel that they have to decide between their career and their children. Ninja Burger is proud to offer day care facilities in each and every franchise location, twenty-four hours a day, seven days a week. Each facility is staffed by a trained ninja who will look after your children as if they were his/her own ninja child.

Our day care facilities include amenities such as:

• Toys and games for all ages, from toddlers to pre-teens
• "Kid Ninja" training in stealth, poisons, and weapon techniques
• Field trips, such as our ever-popular "A Day in the Bear Cage"

FAMILY LEAVE

When necessary (for example, if everyone in your family is not a ninja), our employees may request time off to care for their children (illness, adoption, ninja-teacher conferences, etc.). Employees may also request time off to take care of other family members, such as their spouses or honorable parents.[26]

In all cases, employees are required to use any PTO first, after which TOWP may be taken for a period of up to twelve weeks.

MATERNITY LEAVE

Female ninja (i.e., kunoichi) may request time off for pregnancy, childbirth, or the care of a newborn. PTO must be used first. In the case of maternity leave, this may be supplemented with up to 18 full months of TOWP, not to precede 6 months prior to childbirth, or exceed 12 months after.

Male ninja (i.e., ninja) may also request time off for the care of a newborn. However, male ninja requesting time off for pregnancy or childbirth will be asked to visit a Ninja Burger physician for a physical examination.

25 For more information, see Ninja Pamphlet #69, "That's Not a Sword in My Pocket, But I Am Happy To See You."
26 In fact, if you do NOT request time off to care for your parents, you will be terminated for lack of honor.

OUTSIDE EMPLOYMENT

While Ninja Burger encourages employees to focus entirely on serving their company with total dedication and focus, from time to time workers find it helpful, intriguing, or otherwise necessary to seek simultaneous employment in another job, be that for another business or for oneself.

Our employees are free to engage in other job activities in their time off as long as the work does not interfere with their performance on the job at Ninja Burger or create a conflict of interest. If at any time the other job begins to interfere with Ninja Burger work, the employee will be asked to leave the other job immediately or face termination.

Ninja Burger employees are also forbidden from using Ninja Burger equipment, uniforms, or vehicles for other job duties. If you want to wear a ninja costume to your other job, you'll have to buy your own.[27]

CONFLICTS OF INTEREST

Ninja Burger employees are honor-bound to serve Ninja Burger first and foremost, and to never compromise our secrecy or security. Working for any organizations with whom we directly compete or who are trying to kill us[28] is therefore always forbidden, in order to prevent situations where employees might have their interests conflicted.

Examples of obvious conflicts of interest are:

- Work that interferes with job duties (hours, background checks, etc.)
- Consulting in an area related to work (fast food, ninja stuff, etc.)
- Work for a rival fast-food delivery service (but OK if it's for spying)

While not explicitly forbidden, special approval is needed for the following:

- Work of any kind for a mercenary or black-ops organization
- Acting or stunt work in a ninja-related movie
- Work involving any government entity (they might be customers)

APPROVED JOBS

If the job is not in any of the above categories, and is obviously unrelated to Ninja Burger job duties (food preparation, delivery, killing people), then it does not require approval. Examples include:

- Artistic performance (except mime)
- Farm work (no soy, potato, or beef)
- Running a lemonade stand

You WILL buy
LEMONADE!!!!

$5.00/cup

27 A real ninja would have a spare anyway.
28 And vice-versa.

NINJA BURGER

EMPLOYEE ACTIVITIES TEAM

The Employee Activities Team (E.A.T.) is an employee-run organization that is recognized and supported by Ninja Burger management as a good[29] way of improving morale, relieving stress, and keeping idle hands busy.[30] The E.A.T. schedules recreational activities during off-work hours.

While the team itself is entirely autonomous, Ninja Burger does budget for occasional financial support (see below), and allows for limited and reasonable use of Ninja Burger facilities, vehicles, and property during meetings and approved activities.

ACTIVITY FEES

While participation in E.A.T. functions is entirely voluntary, a nominal activities fee will be deducted from each employee's paycheck to help pay for approved activities. However, this financial support is at the discretion of Ninja Burger management, as advised by the E.A.T. Advisory Panel.

Certain activities (often those not approved for funding) may carry an additional fee (bus fare, hotel accommodations, bribing guards, ammo, etc.). Payment of such fees is the responsibility of the participants.

E.A.T. ADVISORY PANEL

The E.A.T. is headed by an Advisory Panel, consisting of ten members elected by employees to one-year[31] terms. Activities must get a vote from six panel members before they are approved by the panel as a whole.

In addition, two members act in an advisory capacity: one of the two G.O.N.A.D.S., and a permanent E.A.T. Medical Examiner from the Department of Employee and Trainee Health Services. Together the G.O.N.A.D. and the E.A.T. M.E. ensure that activities are acceptable from a health and safety standpoint[32] before they are approved for financial support.

FUNDED ACTIVITIES

Safe and fun activities which are generally encouraged, and almost always approved for financial support, include:

- Bowling (if masks are worn)
- Board, card, and role-playing games
- Slumber parties (not co-ed!)
- Zoo/aquarium/movie/circus trips
- Miniature golf

29 i.e., free. If we don't have to pay for it, it's a good thing.
30 Bored ninja + access to weapons = best avoided.
31 One-year maximum. After particularly ill-attended or unpopular activities, it is common for employees to elect new heads to the panel. Old heads are placed in the trash after removal from the shoulders.
32 Activities deemed too dangerous are still allowed to proceed, and are often among the best-attended each year. Recent examples include: a day with the crocodiles, visiting a volcano, and lawn darts.

HONORABLE EMPLOYEE HANDBOOK

UNFUNDED ACTIVITIES

Activities which are generally discouraged, and usually not approved for financial support, include:

- Bloodsports, dueling, thumb-wrestling[33]
- Racing, drag-racing or racing in drag
- Gambling on the premises or in company vehicles
- Anything involving sharp objects

EMPLOYEE PICNICS

The E.A.T. helps coordinate employee picnics, which are held on a regional basis as schedules allow. These fun picnics allow employees from different franchises to get together to eat, greet, play games, and occasionally fulfill long-standing disputes of honor. As only about half of our employees make it home from any given picnic, such events are generally unfunded.

The E.A.T. is also responsible for the annual Ninja Burger company-wide employee picnic, to which all our employees around the world are invited.[34]

EMPLOYEE COMMUNICATIONS

The E.A.T. publishes a monthly newsletter, *Ninja News*, distributed in both e-mail and print. The newsletter publishes photos, stories, and articles about Ninja Burger, as well as marriage, birth, and death announcements.[35] Employees can contribute to the newsletter via e-mail to aeon@ninjaburger.com.

The E.A.T. (and, indeed, all employees) may also publish communications to other employees using Ninja Burger's bulletin boards (both physical and electronic). However, employees should refrain from posting inappropriate messages in such forums, including vulgar, obscene, or threatening language. Save those for e-mail, please.

33 "Ninja take thumb-wrestling very seriously," says Tetsuo 'Nine-Fingers,' regional champ.
34 However, since they have yet to find a good day when everyone in the world is off work, there has yet to actually be a First Annual Employee Picnic. Maybe next year.
35 For space considerations, death announcements will be posted solely on the web in particularly bad months.

NINJA BURGER

ADVANCED TRAINING

Experienced ninja know their training will never be complete. True ninja are always improving their skills through study, practice, and killing off competitors to make themselves look better. It is our policy to encourage employees who are interested in increasing their knowledge and skill, particularly in areas relevant to their employment. As such, we provide a number of services and facilities to help employees in their search for training.

There are three methods of seeking additional training: management-guided, through the Development Assistance Department, or on your own.

MANAGEMENT-GUIDED TRAINING

In general, your direct supervisor is responsible for identifying areas in which you, as an employee, may wish to work on improving. This is generally done through the general Performance Evaluation Process (described later), though supervisors may request additional training for their employees at any time, whether for skill development or as punishment.[36]

DEVELOPMENT ASSISTANCE DEPARTMENT

The D.A.D. was developed to assist Ninja Burger employees in fulfilling their true potential. The department works with employees on an individual and team basis to determine strengths and weaknesses, and to guide employees towards additional training, which can help them focus on their best skills and eliminate their weaknesses.[37] All employees are welcome to discuss their career plans with the D.A.D. at any time;[38] everyone is welcome.

Under special circumstances, such as when an employee has demonstrated particularly excellent skills and potential, the D.A.D., after consultation with management, may decide to award Ninja Burger employees zero-interest tuition loans for use in seeking training at universities or colleges.

Such loans may vary from a few hundred dollars up to the full cost of tuition, and must be repaid by the employee upon graduation through wage garnishment. Failure to repay the loan is grounds for termination. But at this point in the handbook, that's probably not a surprise.

EMPLOYEE-DIRECTED ADVANCEMENT

In this case, the employee takes the lead in assessing his or her own skills, career interests, and desires, and seeks out training on his or her own. This may involve in-house Ninja Burger facilities (which are always open to employees at all times) or, more commonly, off-site training at universities, colleges, dojos, and secret ninja bases hidden inside volcanoes. Basically, this means you're on your own, so do what you want; just leave us out of it.

36 Often the same thing.
37 Or at least, to do a good job of hiding them.
38 With one restriction: You have to find the D.A.D. first, and we're not telling you where they are. If you cannot find them then you are not a true ninja and are thus not worthy of their time.

CAMPUS FACILITIES

As discussed elsewhere, Ninja Burger training facilities are available for use by all employees at all times for training and practice on a first-come/first-served[39] basis. Facilities vary from franchise to franchise, but all of the following are available to all employees, wherever they might be.

Guide to codes—A: All; F: Franchise; H: Headquarters; R: Regional

- Classrooms (classes vary) (H,R, some F)
- Dojo/practice room (A)
- Weight/cardio room (A)
- Library/reading area (H,R)
- Swimming pool (H,R)
- Petting Zoo (H)

Note that when using Ninja Burger facilities in other franchises or regions, be sure to check with that store's management before sneaking in, so they can disable their security systems[40] before you arrive.

OFF-SITE TRAINING

As befits a global operation, Ninja Burger provides training facilities around the world, everywhere from urban areas to remote wildernesses. Some of these facilities are kept secret to test the mettle of our top ninja, but some of the most popular ones you might want to visit include:

- The Siberian Experience Day Spa
- Sensei Lo-Pan's Temple of Doom
- North Atlantic Free-Diving Center
- Sensei Pai Mei's Mountain Camp
- 1001 Arabian Nights Without Water

OTHER TRAINING

Many employees wish to train at a university, college, or privately held dojo. Students should be aware that many of these organizations are filled with our enemies. Watch out for:

- Pirate Pete-San's Dojo-o'-Fun
- Samurai Sam's Totally Ninja-Friendly Center
- The UC and SUNY university systems

39 Or, if there are schedule conflicts, on a last-one-left-alive basis.
40 Unless, of course, your training involves breaking through their security systems. In which case, don't.

NINJA BURGER

PERFORMANCE EVALUATION PROCESS

All Ninja Burger employees are evaluated on an ongoing basis, day by day, hour by hour, to ensure that their skills and performance are up to standards. As needed, small corrections, advice, and additional training may be added to an employee's schedule to help guide them along.

However, we have found that it is also beneficial to all employees to have quarterly evaluations. These allow us to better track an employee's efforts since the previous evaluation, so that their general performance can be measured, projected, and (if necessary) corrected.

In addition to giving employees feedback, evaluations help Ninja Burger give out raises, bonuses, job transfers, and promotions.[41] They are not to be feared, unless you've been slacking off, in which case you should be afraid.

ONGOING FEEDBACK

Ninja are responsible for ensuring that they are performing their duties to the best of their ability, and for seeking clarification, advice, and input about their performance from their coworkers and managers. Managers should provide helpful, accurate feedback on an ongoing basis. For example:

- "You call that a delivery, Baka? My ancestors could deliver better, and they've been dead for centuries. You are a complete failure."
- "I know it hurts, Sakura, but it'll hurt more if you make me come over there. Now pick up your finger and slice the onion again."
- "Not bad, Toshiro, but next time remove the pit bull from your leg before you complete the delivery. It'll save five, maybe ten seconds."
- "Tanaka, this customer has been on hold for three seconds already. Unacceptable. Remove your left pinky finger as a reminder."

QUARTERLY EVALUATIONS

Every ninety days, all supervisors are required to provide—in writing—an evaluation of that employee's performance. One copy should be given to the Ninja Archives, and a second copy to the employee.

An honest appraisal of the employee's performance must be contained in each copy of the evaluation, as well as any recommendations for a salary increase, bonus, promotions, transfer to another department, or termination.[42]

---

41 Not to mention they also provide blackmail material.
42 If the employee is being recommended for termination, it is usually advisable to provide that employee a slightly less-honest version of the evaluation, to keep them off-guard. They're much easier to terminate when they don't expect it.

SALARY AND JOB ADJUSTMENTS

Changes to a ninja's salary or work duties may be made at any time. But in accordance with our "ongoing feedback" policy, such adjustments are generally made on a quarterly basis following scheduled evaluations. At that time, based on the recommendation of an employee's manager, any adjustments to hourly pay rate or changes of position will be instituted.

In addition, ninja employees are welcome and even encouraged to submit, in writing, any requests for salary or job changes based on performance, need or desire.[43] Such requests may be made about oneself or coworkers.

CHANGES IN PAY RATE

In addition to regular annual adjustments to the base hourly rate to keep up with the marketplace, a ninja's salary may be adjusted on a quarterly basis. These salary adjustments are generally made based on merit—rewarding employees who have been working diligently, showing improvement, or helping to improve company profits.

Adjustments may also be made based on need, but don't count on it.

Please note that in the event of negative performance, your salary can never be adjusted downwards except in cases where it's reduced right to zero; if you're performing that badly, you'll just be terminated.

JOB TRANSFERS

Based on the recommendation of their manager, employees may transfer between departments or to a higher position in their department.

All changes must be approved by the ninja's manager, except in cases where the employee is replacing their ninja manager through direct means,[44] in which case the employee may approve his or her own advancement.

RELOCATION EXPENSES

As Ninja Burger prefers to keep employees on familiar turf, there will be little need for relocation under most circumstances. However, in the event that an employee must relocate (e.g., promotion, transfer to another franchise, or transfer to "get you out of our hair"), we cover relocation costs as follows:

- One (1) coach-class ticket on an airline of Ninja Burger's choice, not to include baggage above and beyond the airline's normal limits.
- Air-sickness medication, or crystallized ginger, if needed for nausea.
- Free mandatory elimination of all belongings and other evidence left behind, via incineration (or other means, as appropriate).
- Optional elimination of all witnesses left behind (at employee cost); employees are encouraged to "clean up" their own messes.

---

43 It won't make any difference, but these provide entertaining reading material for Ninja Burger managers.
44 e.g., poisoning, knifing, etc.

NINJA BURGER

PROBLEM RESOLUTION

Ninja Burger's goal is to provide a workplace in which all our employees can flourish. So when problems arise we do our best to deal with them promptly and appropriately, allowing all involved parties to quickly sort out their differences, so they can put the problem behind them.

The basic problem resolution process is as follows:

1. Employee reports a problem.
2. Problem is investigated.
3. If there is a problem, the problem is dealt with. If there is not a problem, the employee becomes the problem and is dealt with.
4. Problem resolution is reported to employee. If employee was the problem, then resolution is reported to employee's next of kin.

REPORTING PROBLEMS

If a Ninja Burger employee has a problem that directly affects them only, such as a particular working condition, pay rate, job duties, or problem with a specific employee, they should contact their supervisor,[45] who will help them find an appropriate method of dealing with the problem, such as:

• Take care of it himself.

In the event that a supervisor is unable to assist an employee in solving a personal problem, upper management will deal with the employee directly, assuming you can track them down. They are ninja, after all.

CORRECTIVE ACTION

Occasionally, often as a direct result of a quarterly evaluation, an employee is determined to be the source of a problem. Such problems might include: inattentiveness, failure to follow directions, poor performance, insubordination, chronic MIA status, chronic lateness, or any other behavior which could conflict with Ninja Burger policies.[46]

Corrective action to correct, punish, or eliminate such behavior is at the discretion of Ninja Burger management, and may include: written warnings, demotion, suspension without pay, corrective action (loss of fingers), or (if necessary) termination (discussed on the last page of this guide).

Documentation of the corrective action taken should be placed in the employee's records along with the reason for the correction. After a year, employees may request in writing that any problems involving them (along with records of corrective action taken) may be purged from their records.[47]

---

45 Unless, of course, their supervisor is the problem, in which case they're so totally screwed.
46 Please note that problems do not include: violence, acts endangering others, possession of weapons, dishonesty, or similar things. Such things are expected of employees and are generally cause for reward, not punishment.
47 All such requests will be ignored, but employees may still make them if they wish.

74

WORKPLACE HARASSMENT

As has been explained earlier, Ninja Burger does not discriminate against employees for any reason. This official policy applies to all employees.

Harassment consists of unwelcome conduct of any kind, including derogatory comments, ethnic slurs, dirty jokes, or teasing and badgering.

We do not tolerate such discriminatory conduct or harassment of any kind against employees based on age, height, weight, race, creed, color, national origin, religion, gender, sexual preference, marital status, ancestry, gender identity, pregnancy, physical or mental disability, medical condition, citizenship, status as a veteran, or political affiliation.

However, the harassment policy is exempted during the first week of an employee's hiring, during which time we allow reasonable hazing[48] as part of a team-building experience. Silly newbie.

SEXUAL HARASSMENT

Since all employees wear ninja uniforms and masks, sexual harassment is generally not a problem, as there is less "visual enticement." However, it does happen, and it deserves special attention here.

Ninja Burger does not tolerate any unwelcome sexual advances or sexual harassment, be they between employees of the same or opposite sex.

To clarify, sexual harassment is any unwelcome conduct that is sexually based, which may include: sexual propositions, innuendo, lewd or obscene jokes, suggestive or racy comments, rude gestures, or sexually driven contact such as unwanted hugging, kissing, patting, pinching, or rubbing.

Ninja Burger will take corrective action when necessary. However, we wish to point out that female ninja (kunoichi) are masters of small, sharp objects and poisons, and often deal with harassment in a more direct fashion.

48 Reasonably defined as anything that won't permanently injure, incapacitate, or kill.

Ninja Burger

Termination

The good thing about this *Honorable Employee Handbook* is that the sections on retirement, premature death, and termination of employees all fit on the same page. That's because they all fall under the same basic policy: You can never be fired from Ninja Burger—only terminated.

Termination may come about due to a poor evaluation, disregard for company policy, failure to deliver in 30 minutes or less, attempting to quit, etc. All terminations fall into two categories: voluntary and involuntary.

Resignations

Ninja Burger has no exit policy, and as such all employees are deemed to be employees for life. Should you decide that you no longer wish to work for Ninja Burger, you may decide to voluntarily terminate. Should you opt not to self-terminate, then your termination will be dubbed involuntary.

Involuntary Termination

Employees who attempt to leave the company or who engage in behavior that conflicts with Ninja Burger policy will be involuntarily terminated. This termination policy begins with verbal notice of termination, followed by a written notice placed in the employee's file. Then the employee is hunted down by a team of trained assassins and terminated.

Voluntary Termination (Seppuku)

Employees may also choose to make things easier on themselves and voluntarily terminate through seppuku. This is the honorable way to go about it:

1. Find a friend to be a "Kaishakunin" (or "second").
2. Find a sharp knife. Preferably, a kozuka; but a tanto, wakizashi, or katana will do in a pinch. Not a spatula.
3. Kneel down. Drink some sake. It'll help. Trust us.
4. Reach down and grab your weapon. If your second is paying attention, at this point they'll see that you're committed to the action and will slice off your head, saving you a lot of pain with a quick "coup de grâce."
5. If you're still alive, your goal is to restore your honor through painful disembowelment. Get to it.
6. When you're done, your second cuts off your head. Disregard if your head was previously cut off in step 4.

Severance Pay

Severance pay, if it is due, will be made to the employee's next of kin, upon evidence that the employee's head has actually been severed.

APPENDIX A: TEMPORARY ID CARD

The following pages contain handouts, quick reference guides, and other information that while not directly relevant to *The Honorable Employee Handbook* may still be of use to Ninja Burger employees. You have permission to copy these Appendix pages, numbered A through L, as needed.

You will not copy other parts of the Guide or you will DIE!

TEMPORARY ID CARD
Cut on the lines and keep in your wallet.

NINJA BURGER EMPLOYEE
TEMPORARY IDENTIFICATION CARD
#00000001

Name: _____

Address: _____

Gender: _____ Hair: _____
Height: _____ Eyes: _____
Weight: _____ DOB: _____

TEMPORARY PARKING PERMIT
Cut on the lines and keep on your dashboard.

NINJA BURGER EMPLOYEE
TEMPORARY PARKING PERMIT
#00000001

Name: _____

Employee #: _____

License Plate #: _____

Make: _____ Model: _____

NINJA BURGER

INSTRUCTIONS

The temporary identification card and parking permit herein are intended to be used only until your permanent ID card and permit are provided by the Archives Department. Employees found using these temporary documents beyond an initial grace period of several days will find that they no longer need them. Because they will be dead.

TEMPORARY ID CARD

Cut on the lines and keep in your wallet.

> THIS IS AN ILLEGALLY BINDING DOCUMENT
> According to the guidelines of the Ninja Burger Anatomical Gift Act, the bearer of this card does hereby agree, upon his/her death, to:
>
> A X Donate all of my organs, tissues or parts
> B X Donate any implants or cybernetic bits
> C X Donate my body, to be carved up for bits
>
> For X Transplant   X Research   X Whatever
>
> Signed: _____
> (signature not necessary; possession of this card confirms assent)

TEMPORARY PARKING PERMIT

Cut on the lines and keep on your dashboard.

> LIMITATION OF LIABILITY. The bearer of this card (or the owner of the car for which this permit is being used) agrees not to hold Ninja Burger liable for any theft or damages that may occur while the vehicle is parked on Ninja Burger property.
>
> This permit is valid while the vehicle is parked in the lot of the assigned franchise, or any other franchise, to which the employee has been temporarily assigned. In all cases, this permit will expire two weeks from the date the employee first used it. Use after that date will result in towing.
>
> Vehicles parked more than 24 hours in one spot will be towed at owner expense. Vehicles may be recovered from the bottom of the nearest lake.
>
> Signed: _____
> (signature not necessary; possession of this card confirms assent)

NINJA BURGER EMPLOYMENT FORM

Name/Alias: _____

Social Security #: (No need to enter this—we already know it.)

Street Address: _____

Village: _____ Prefecture: _____

Phone #: _____ E-mail:_____

Are You 18?   Yes   No
Are You Immortal?   Yes   No   So Far

Have You Ever Been a Samurai,
Ninja, or Other Bushi Before?   Yes   No   Maybe

If Yes, Daimyo: _____

Reason for Going Ronin: Dishonor   Daimyo killed

HOURS AVAILABLE:

	Mon.	Tue.	Wed.	Thu.	Fri.	Sat.	Sun.
From							
To							

Total Hours Available Per Week: _____

Are You Under a Curse,
Geas, or Blood Oath?   Yes   No   Curse Prevents from Saying

How Did You Hear Of Job? _____

How Far Do You Live From Ninja Burger? _____ Miles / KM

How Will You Get To Work?   Horse   Run   Ninja Magic

NINJA BURGER

DOJO MOST RECENTLY ATTENDED:

Name: _____

Street Address: _____

Village: _____ Prefecture: _____

Phone #: _____ Martial Art: _____

Sensei: _____ Kyu/Dan: _____

Reason for Leaving: Dishonor   Sensei Killed
                         Graduated   Defeated Sensei in Single Combat

---

TWO MOST RECENT JOBS:

Employer: _____

Street Address: _____

Village: _____ Prefecture: _____

Phone #: _____ Payment: _____

Dates Worked: From _____ To _____

Reason for Leaving: Dishonor   Mission Completed
                         Killed Employer   Betrayed by Employer, Killed Him

Employer: _____

Street Address: _____

Village: _____ Prefecture: _____

Phone #: _____ Payment: _____

Dates Worked: From _____ To _____

Reason for Leaving: Dishonor   Mission Completed
                         Killed Employer   Betrayed by Employer, Killed Him

APPENDIX B: APPLICATION

Ninja Burger is an equal opportunity employer committed to a diverse work force. In order to assist us in our efforts, we invite you to voluntarily provide responses to the following requests for information. Failure to respond will result in you involuntarily providing responses to the following requests for information. This form will be kept strictly confidential and will not be retained with your employment application, even though it is on the other side of the same sheet of paper as your application. By reading this paragraph you have accepted Ninja Burger's terms and agree to cooperate.

Sex: Male   Female

Race/Color/National Origin: Japanese   Chinese   Korean
                                 Vietnamese   Taiwanese   American

If American, do you own *Gymkata* on VHS or DVD?   Yes   No
(If "Yes," we are sorry, but we cannot take your application seriously. We suggest you try Samurai Burger.)

Ninja Burger provides a unique service to our customers. This service may include situations which could prove quite hazardous to your health, or the health of others. These situations include: capture by the enemy; attack by ronin or samurai warriors; poison by rogue ninja; temptation by nubile female ninja; falling off walls; falling into spiked pits; being decapitated; grease burns; and salmonella poisoning. By signing below (not optional), you agree to hold Ninja Burger free of all liability regarding any injury or death which may occur during the above, or any other, circumstances which may or may not arise as a condition of working for Ninja Burger. Furthermore, you agree that Ninja Burger will deny your employment if asked by anyone, including future employers, law enforcement officials, or next of kin.

Sign Here: _____

During the past ten years, have you ever been convicted of or pled guilty to a crime, excluding misdemeanors and traffic violations?   Yes   No

If Yes, why were you captured?

During the past ten years, have you ever committed a crime/crimes for which you were not convicted?   Yes   No

If Yes, describe in full:

NINJA BURGER

MILITARY EEPERIENCE:

Branch of Service: _____

Country: _____

Dates Worked: From _____   To _____

Rank: _____   Payment: _____

Reason for Leaving: Dishonor   Mission Completed
                       Killed Employer   Betrayed by Employer, Killed Him

Branch of Service: _____

Country: _____

Dates Worked: From _____   To _____

Rank: _____   Payment: _____

Reason for Leaving: Dishonor   Mission Completed
                       Killed Employer   Betrayed by Employer, Killed Him

GENERAL EXPERIENCE:
What additional relevant experiences or training have you had which you feel would add to your value as a Ninja Burger employee? (Include weapons, poisons, or any of the Ninja Juhakkei):

I certify that I have read and fully completed both sides of this application and that the information contained on this application is correct to the best of my knowledge and understand that any omission or erroneous information is grounds for dismissal, torture, or decapitation by Ninja Burger. I acknowledge that Ninja Burger reserves the right to amend or modify the policies at any time, without prior notice, and that these policies do not create any promises or contractual obligations between Ninja Burger and its employees. At Ninja Burger, employment is not at will. This means I am not free to terminate my employment at any time, for any reason. Attempts to terminate employment will result in death.

Sign Here: _____

NINJA BURGER®
DELIVERY MENU

ORDER ONLINE 24 HOURS A DAY AT
HTTP://WWW.NINJABURGER.COM

ITEM	DESCRIPTION	PRICE
1. Ninja Burger	Our specialty. Two soy-meat patties hand-broiled in the traditions of our ancestors, special sauce, lettuce, cheese, pickles, onions, and Kung-Fu Grip! All in a roll.	$3.50 (¥374)
2. Double Ninja Burger	Four soy-meat patties cooked over an open flame fueled by the bones of our enemies, special sauce, lettuce, cheese, pickles, onions, and Kung-Fu Grip. All in a roll.	$5.50 (¥588)
3. Junior Ninja Burger	One soy-meat patty with special sauce, cheese, pickles and onions (no lettuce or Kung-Fu Grip), in a roll.	$2.00 (¥214)
4. Samurai Chicken Sandwich	Get it? Samurai chicken? Hahaha. Erk. Does not contain real samurai (stupid FDA regulations), but does contain a spicy coating, lettuce, tomato, and wasabi sauce.	$3.50 (¥374)
5. French Fries of Our Ancestors	Crispy french fries cooked in a secret Ninja Burger style, sprinkled with a secret selection of spices.	$2.50 (¥267)
6. Onion Death Blossom	Specially requested by our ninja friends down under. Sliced by katana and deep-fried. It's ninjariffic!	$5.50 (¥588)
7. Large Cola	Were you expecting sake? We do not offer sake. When we offer sake, old gaijin lady, spill hot sake on lap. Sue Ninja Burger for million yen. You drink cola! Cola good enough for ninja, and it is good enough for you, too.	$1.50 (¥160)
8. Ninja Burger Combo Meal #1	Ninja Burger, French Fries of Our Ancestors, and Large Cola. Do not ask for better perfection because there is none, also we would kill you for asking. Enjoy!	$7.00 (¥756)
9. Ninja Burger Combo Meal #2	Double Ninja Burger, French Fries of Our Ancestors, and Large Cola. Meal made for a sumo, or a large Ninja!	$9.00 (¥972)

Ohashi, wasabi, and napkins (serviettes) are included free of charge with every order, but a minimum of $10 (¥1,068) must be spent with every order or we will mock you. And please keep in mind that although Ninja Burger provides free delivery in most areas, a nominal delivery charge may be applied depending on your delivery location. Finally, no, we do NOT serve fortune cookie with food. Fortune cookie is Chinese. Ninja Burger is Japanese. Stupid gaijin.

Ninja Burger

THE NINJA NEWS
SEPTEMBER 2005

FIRST THINGS FIRST

Welcome once again to yet another exciting edition of the *Ninja News*.

We'd like to thank both of our readers for taking the time to comment on our last issue. As you can see, we've updated our look, and hired a new editor to replace S████████████n, who was terminated for poor editing skills. We wish the best of luck to new editor, ████████████.

PHOTO CONTEST WINNERS

Last month we asked you to submit photographs of your Ninja Burger franchises, paying attention to color, contrast, lighting, and secrecy. This month we announce our winners.

Congrats to our winner, ████████ ████████ at franchise #175 in ████████████, and lucky runner-up ████████████ at franchise #2043! Their winning entries are below.

For winning the contest, ████████-san will receive a coupon good for a free Onion Death Blossom. And for coming in second place, ████-san will commit seppuku. Tough break!

WHAT'S HAPPENING?

• Last month, Ninja Burger again exceeded sales records, bringing in $14,247,013 in revenues, matched against costs of $3,830,218. Top losses were antiseptics (15 percent), burial costs (22 percent), payoffs (11 percent) and extra wasabi (4 percent) from our special Sumo-Size Your Wasabi customer promotion (now over).

• The increasingly popular Ninja Burger Web site drew an estimated 29,000 new customers last week, moving it up to second place in order placement (first being phone, third being carrier pigeon).

• Employee turnover remained stable once again, with 5,073 new hires worldwide versus 1,953 deaths and 3,103 terminations.

• Franchise #13 once again burned to the ground after fire swept through the grill area, killing all employees. Plans to rebuild the franchise are being drawn up, this time with advanced safety features like smoke detectors, fire extinguishers, and doors.

• We've discontinued our latest Kids' Meal giveaway due to customer feedback. Stores should destroy any extra stock of the "Make a Ninja Mask from a Plastic Bag" promo.

• Franchise #1863 reports suspicious activity around Samurai Burger #103. "It sounds like digging," says one employee. Be alert!

NINJA BURGER

COMINGS & GOINGS

• WE WILL MISS ██████████, our long-time keeper of carrier pigeons, who died last month after learning that he had fallen to third place in orders. Cause of death was believed to be seppuku. ██ is survived by a wife and two children, the elder of which is expected to avenge his father's death any day now.

• WELCOME ████████████ first born son of employee #17283 ████████████. Little ██████-san has his mother's eyes, his father's strength, and his grandfather's spirit. He'll need it, since he's destined to defeat a great evil on his eighteenth birthday!

• CONGRATULATIONS to ████████████ who finally tracked down the samurai who killed his entire family in cold blood. On a sad note, ████ committed seppuku immediately after completing his debt of honor, but we're sure that he rests with his ancestors.

• BETRAYED by Takanaka Wataba-san. This unworthy, dishonorable dog left our employ to work for a competitor (rhymes with Vendy's) without properly terminating. If you see him, use caution in ending his life.

Let Us Know! Send your birth, death and marriage annoucements via email to aeon@ninjaburger.com

KATANA KORNER
(continued from last month)
By now you've got your fire nice and hot again, so it's time to heat up that blade. Get it nice and white hot, then while it's still glowing, pound it flat and fold the edges on themselves to create the 97th layer. Not too much! You're going for strength here, true, but a bit too much strength now will weaken the blade later.

Next week: The crucial 98!

NINJA PUZZLER
The ninja chefs forgot to slice the bun like the customers said. If three customers are sharing the burger, can you chop the bun equally with two katana slices?

Last Week's Puzzle Solution:
Kambei teams with Kyuzo, Shino teams with Kikuchiyo, Gorobei teams with Rikichi, Heihachi teams with Shichiroji, and Manzo teams with Yohei. Congratulations to ████████████n from franchise #2036, our only winner.

FALL PICNIC PHOTOS!
Fall for our North American franchises means it's time for picnics. Some of the employees from franchise #1712 sent us these photos from their recent get-together. Looks like fun! Too bad they all had to commit seppuku for releasing these to us.

Organizational Chart

HEADQUARTERS
Dir. A███████████   Dir.███████████

Chairman ███████████
Co-Chairperson ███████

Board of Supervisors
███
███

- -

REGION (N. America, Eurasia, S. America, Pac. Rim)
Regional Director ███████████████

President of Operations ███████████████

V.P. Operations ███████████████

- -

COUNTRY (U.S.A., Canada, France, Uzbekistan, etc.)
National Director ███████████

Co-Director ███████████████

Government Liaison ███████████████

- -

SECTOR (Western U.S., Ontario, Northern Japan, etc.)
Sector Head ███████████

Sector Operational Specialist ███████████

- -

ZONE (N. California, Manhattan, Ile de France, etc.)
Zone Chief ███████████

- -

FRANCHISE (#1)
Franchise Manager ███████████████

Head Chef ███████████████

Head of Dispatch ███████████

NINJA BURGER

EMPLOYEE CONTACT LIST

HEADQUARTERS
Main Number: 1-(415)-██████ ext. 101
Main e-mail: aeon@ninjaburger.com

Central Dispatch
    Customers: 1-(800)-██████
    Employee Hotline: 1-(415)-██████
Employee Resources
    Ninja Archive Division (N.A.D.): 1-(415)-██████ ext. 107
    Dept. of Employee & Trainee
        Health Services (D.E.A.T.H.): 1-(415)-██████ ext. 109
    Development Assistance Dept. (D.A.D.): 1-(415)-8█████ext. 203
Communications & Marketing
    Government Liaison: 1-(415)-██████ ext. 333
    Public Relations: 1-(415)-██████ ext. 337
    Marketing: 1-(415)-██████ ext. 331
    Advertising: 1-(415)-██████ ext. 332
    Graphic Design: 1-(415)-██████ ext. 339
    Web Design: 1-(415)-██████ ext. 338
Security: 1-(415)-██████ ext. 999
    Armory: 1-(415)-██████ ext. 909
Administration & Finance
    Finance: 1-(415)-██████ ext. 408
    Purchasing: 1-(415)-██████ ext. 407
IT Department
    Security Center: 1-(415)-██████ ext. 644
    Network Operations Center: 1-(415)-██████ ext. 664
    Clean Room: 1-(415)-██████ ext. 666
Ninja Burger Recruitment: 1-(415)-██████ ext. 911

FRANCHISES
Main Number: 1-(area code)-██████ ext. 101
Kitchen: 1-(area code)-██████ ext. 200
    Head Chef (cell): 1-(area code)-██████
    Test Kitchen: 1-(area code)-██████ ext. 221
Delivery
    Garage: 1-(area code)-██████ ext. 500
    Locker Room: 1-(area code)-██████ ext. 543
Day Care: 1-(area code)-██████ ext. 707

OTHER
Any Vehicle (cell): 101 + Vehicle ID Number (VIN)
Any Employee (cell): 101 + Employee ID Number (EIN)
Any Employee e-mail: (codename)@ninjaburger.com

Notes

To Do!
- ~~Get ninja outfit from dry cleaners~~
- ~~Sharpen ninja stars~~
- Pick up kids from school
- Take van in for oil change
- Avenge father's murder

Groceries!
Ketchup & Mustard
Hamburger buns
Hamburg. meat
Chese
Pickle Rellish
Toilet Paper
Cat food
Dog food
Leopard food
Cleaning Stuff (what gets blood out of carpet???)

Work Schedule!
Sunday! 8am – 6pm
Monday! 9am – 10pm
Tuesday! 12am – 10pm
Wednesday! 2am – 6pm
Thrsday! 12am – 11pm
Friday! 1am – 9pm
Saturday! ~~OFF!~~   12am – 10pm

NOTES

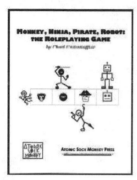

91